KNIT

LAURENCE KING

Published in 2015 by
Laurence King Publishing Ltd
361–363 City Road, London,
EC1V 1LR, United Kingdom
T +44 (0)20 7841 6900
F + 44 (0)20 7841 6910
enquiries@laurenceking.com
www.laurenceking.com

This book was produced by Laurence King Publishing Ltd, London

A catalogue record for this book is available from the British Library

ISBN 978-1-78067-472-8

Design by Shaz Madani

Printed in China

Front cover: Leutton Postle, Spring/Summer 2013 Collection, photo by Simon Armstrong

KNIT: Innovations in Fashion, Art, Design

Samantha Elliott

Laurence King Publishing

Contents

Introduction

Knit: Innovations in Fashion, Art, Design aims to present a snapshot of what is happening globally within knit, capturing the zeitgeist by exploring the multitude of outcomes being produced by fashion designers, product designers, artists and community knitters (guerrilla knitters, knitting groups, charities and others) who choose knit to realize their visions. The interviews they provide cover a range of issues, including design philosophy, the creative process, aesthetics, materials, technologies, environmental influences, and stitch and yarn choices.

The contributors featured have all been recognized for the quality of their work, whether they are up-and-coming young designers, or well-established companies that have been trading for hundreds of years. What they also have in common is the desire to work with knit in a highly innovative way, either through design or technology – or both. Wherever possible, contributors have been asked to provide imagery that has not been published before, resulting in a fresh and exciting selection of pictures that illustrate environment, process and outcome.

There are a few fantastic publications already in existence that explore knitting in its many forms, but there are not many. As well as adding to their number, I believe this book offers a fresh approach, demonstrating the versatility of knit by grouping current practitioners into three different disciplines, inviting the reader to compare and contrast. The approach of anarchic, forward thinking design label Sibling, for example, can be seen alongside the work of Ruth Marshall, an artist who studies and recreates rare or extinct animal pelts through knitting, and the performance pieces, or 'knit interventions', staged by Liz Collins in the USA. While very different in their approach and their outcomes, they nevertheless all share the drive to produce original and thought-provoking work.

In fact, while interviewing the contributors, what struck me were the similarities between them. I asked Toshiko Horiuchi MacAdam how she defined herself, and her response was that this was something that probably mattered more to other people than to her. This is perhaps true of all the contributors; many could go in any section as they demonstrate such broad and diverse practice.

In the 1980s, knitting experienced a sharp decline. Sales of yarns and knitting patterns dropped massively as interest in the craft was replaced by fast fashion and the wide availability of cheap machine-knitted garments. However, as part of a resurgent interest in crafting in the twenty-first century, and benefitting from the development of the internet, knitting is now enjoying a revival. Memberships of guilds and clubs are increasing rapidly (the Women's Institute expects to have 250,000 members by the end of 2015), with members wanting to forge contacts with like-minded practitioners both in the real and virtual world. The local yarn store has been reinstated. Knitting suits our time. It is no longer an essential skill performed by a housewife to create cheaper garments (cheap garments are readily available, and yarn is no longer cheap by comparison), but a craft of choice, enabling makers and doers to develop skills, express a design aesthetic, make a political statements and become members of a community.

Knitters have also embraced the online world, with websites such as Stitch 'n' Bitch encouraging knitters to set up groups, and Ravelry (which had 3 million members in 2013) offering a user-driven knit and crochet community. Knitters can now use the internet to learn from each other, blog, and share information and inspiration, creating the ultimate global knitting group.

Guerrilla knitting has been embraced as a global activity, too, with yarn bombing (or 'graffiti knitting') taking place on every continent. Some of these interventions are domestic in scale, affecting a handful of people who may pass an embellished tree or lamppost on the way to work. Others have a larger political presence, magnifying the inadequacy of a public space, or drawing attention to important issues such as homophobia or nuclear disarmament. Sadly, this movement may possibly have become a victim of its own success, having been adopted as a marketing tool by large companies. However, there are a number of practitioners who are undergoing a rebranding of their own and are reclaiming the activity, creating works that both provoke thought and demonstrate technical excellence.

Technology has also developed to enable faster, more efficient and (when pushed by an inspirational designer or artist) innovative knitting. And yarn development continues to evolve: a huge industry supports spinners and trend forecasters; global fairs showcase technical developments in spinning and construction, and are well attended by designers, corporations and fashion and textile students. Yarns can be strong – strong enough even to support the weight of the human body, or bodies, as with the play structures of Toshiko Horiuchi MacAdam – enabling artists to explore ideas related to scale and human interaction. Or they can be super-fine, able to create the most fragile, web-like structures.

Knit has been reinterpreted into products, too – scaled up to perform weight-bearing tasks as furniture, see Claire-Anne O'Brien in the design section, or as fine ceramics as cast by award-winning designer Annette Bugansky; knitted homewares exist designed to satisfy our need for nostalgia, or reinterpreted for our modern age with up-to-date colours that fit into our homes and comfort our children.

Knitting continues to inspire, inform and surprise. I hope you identify with some of the practitioners showcased in this book, and that they inspire you to be bolder, more experimental, and to continue engaging with a skill that has been evolving for thousands of years.

9.

Fashion

Fashion is a huge, multifaceted industry and, for many, the preferred platform for the knitted structure. This section attempts to capture current trends by presenting a few of today's most inspirational designers and companies. There are notable exceptions. One may ask, why have a fashion section if it does not include the big brands? My feeling was that their work already receives a lot of coverage, so I have chosen instead to focus on designers who are ones to watch – promising underground creatives, or those demonstrating particularly innovative techniques and styling.

The British design duo Alice Lee create luxury garments, with all pieces knitted entirely on a domestic knitting machine, pushing the technology to its limits. These are hands-on designers who will knit on the machine for hours to craft amazingly intricate structures.

Rising star Christian Wijnants is the first of two winners of the esteemed International Woolmark Prize to be featured in this book. The second is Sibling, a trio known for their unconventional reinterpretation of such classic knitted pieces as the twinset, using bright colours and luxurious embellishments.

Relative newcomers Leutton Postle discuss their love of developing knitted fabrics, driven by a passion for colour and textiles, alongside fellow London designer Markus Lupfer – known for his embellished motif sweaters, adored by celebrities and often copied by mainstream retailers.

Canadian Mark Fast is renowned for his construction skills. His approach to knitted clothing embraces this decade's love of body-conscious, or 'bodycon', clothing to celebrate the female form.

Ramón Gurillo is a Spanish designer and passionate advocate of knitting. Fuelled by a love of his country, his clothes resonate with nostalgia and warmth.

In this section we also discuss wider social implications with fashion-industry professionals. Ian Maclean from John Smedley – arguably the oldest factory in the world – discusses plans for the future and the reasons why his family business has remained a mayor player in the fashion world. Masaki Karasuno, from the Japanese manufacturer Shima Seiki, explains how technological innovations, such as their WholeGarment technology, are leading design breakthroughs.

And finally, Rob Langtry from Woolmark discusses how the core values of quality, innovation and respect for the environment have enabled his organization to remain at the forefront of global design, while encompassing avenues as diverse as trend prediction, educational programmes, designer collaborations and sponsorship awards.

10.

Alice Lee

Husband-and-wife duo Alice Smith and Lee Farmer worked together on projects for several global design companies before forming their own knitwear label, Alice Lee. Respected for their attention to detail, they create beautifully made pieces on a domestic knitting machine, often pushing the technique of partial knitting.

Alice Lee were recipients of the British Fashion Council's Newgen scheme for three consecutive seasons in 2001–2, and were one of Vauxhall Fashion Scout's Ones to Watch in 2012. The label was also included by Selfridges in their 2012 Bright Young Things line-up, which resulted in a window display at the famous London store. The duo describe themselves as having a 'couture aesthetic with a modern edge'.

What are your roles within the company?

We design and create the collection together, but we each have our specific roles. Lee is responsible for drawing/illustrating and developing our ideas on paper and in 3D patterns. My focus (Alice) is on fabric and knit development, and production of samples. We work together to finalise each piece and the collections, and to run the studio and manage production.

How would you describe the design philosophy behind Alice Lee?

We produce knitted garments that are finished to an extremely high level, and the silhouette is often driven by the materials and hand techniques used. Attention to highly developed surface design and use of little-known craft techniques is a key aspect of the design process.

It is important to us at the moment that our work is made in the UK so that we can keep a close eye on our production and quality control. Lee also has a background in leather and this is evident in the finishing of some of our pieces.

Can you describe your creative thinking process, and how this is realized as products?

We always start with the knitted fabric, and we often work with our fabrics on the stand (mannequin) to develop silhouette. We may rework old favourites or best-sellers, and push our ideas to resolve and improve ideas, embellish and/or finalize the knitted fabrics to fit the season. We have favourite yarns, which we know are successful on the gauge we knit to.

At what stage of the design process do you consider materials and technologies?

Knitting comes first; we start with yarn and fabric. All our knitted stitches are created using a domestic knit machine, which some people find hard to believe, and we are convinced we have tried every technique possible on those machines. I find that it is really creative, as you can see and feel the knit growing. I also keep extensive notes to pass on to the production knitters. I'm always experimenting with new mixes of yarns and techniques to create our own textiles.

Do you find working in a partnership challenging or beneficial?

It works for us – we are partners in life as well as in business. We bring different skills and experiences to the table, but have a strong mutual respect for each other's working process.

Who has inspired you the most?

We work instinctively, taking inspiration from anything and everything – any kind of design – although most of the time it is art and not other fashion designers. It can also come from something abstract like a feeling or an idea or an image. We don't start with a concept, and have never given a collection a name.

How do you see the Alice Lee label developing?

We are working with an agent to reach a broader client base, and we aim to push into different markets whilst still retaining a strong brand identity, keeping the Alice Lee core values and design signature evident.

11.

1

Fashion: Alice Lee

3

4

1. Full-circle check dress with integrated leather stitching. Lee Farmer's background in leather design is evident in many Alice Lee designs.

2. This stand-out dress embraces a multitude of holding techniques possible with the domestic knitting machine. It showcases not only the versatility of the machine, but also the expertise of the designer and the skills of the makers.

3. Intricate leather lacework draws attention to the sleeves of this dress.

4. One of Alice Lee's favourite techniques is to employ a mix of materials. This piece is an effective combination of leather panels and knit.

6

7

5. White dress holding rippled leather lacework.

6. Alice Lee's versatile use of techniques also extends to the design of accessories, such as these delicate socks.

7. Leather lacework adds shape to and enhances the silhouette of this broken-check dress, made from embroidered knit.

8

9

8. Leather panels and yarn are artfully combined here to create clean-cut yet interesting separates.

9. The direction of the knit has been cleverly considered by the designers for their Stephanie Dress. It has been adjusted so that it gently hugs the body, with added fullness in the skirt.

10. A clean silhouette was achieved with these separates by using fine-gauge knit, with leather lacework providing added detail.

17.

10

Ornella Bignami

Ornella Bignami set up the research and trend forecasting company Elementi Moda in 1979. She is a leading expert on yarn, colour, lifestyle, fashion direction and material. Ornella has earned a wide credibility within her field, and is a member of leading trend groups such as Première Vision, Intercolor and Color Coloris. She also acts as Trend Consultant for colour and material innovation for the Deutsches Mode-Institut (German Fashion Institute) and the European Confederation of Linen and Hemp (CELC).

Ornella's work now also includes facilitating collaborations between industry and education – Feel the Yarn, and FIT in Milan (a programme enabling students of New York's Fashion Institute of Technology to split their training between Milan and New York).

What is your role within the company?

My function, apart from being the founder of the company, is to define the company's strategies, operating as art director in researching personally the new trends and coordinating the activities of a staff of designers.

Can you describe a typical day's work?

There is no typical day's work for me, as I am often travelling to visit exhibitions, meet customers, or working in the office, always on more than one project at a time.

Collaboration must be very important to your work. What are the key ingredients in a successful collaboration?

Collaboration succeeds when you can supply innovative ideas, feasible projects in time with the consumers' market, and work closely with your customer team.

What do you see as the key strengths of the knitting industry?

Emerging strengths within the knitting industry are the use of innovative production technologies ('total garments' and 'seamless knits'), but also the renewed interest in hand-knitted, crafted production, reconnecting the consumer with the humanity of traditional inspiration and natural materials.

What is the most successful project you have worked on, and do you have a favourite?

In all these years I have had the opportunity to experience numerous successful projects. However, one of the most recent initiatives is Feel the Yarn, backed by Toscana Promozione, the economic promotion agency for the Tuscany region, in collaboration with Pitti Immagine and the Consorzio Promozione Filati (Yarn Promotion Consortium).

Feel the Yarn is a training project and competition for knitwear designers from the most prestigious international fashion and design schools. It aims to expand their knowledge of the yarns being produced by the most qualified Italian spinners. The garments designed for the competition are exhibited in a dedicated area during Pitti Filati and voted on by a technical jury and exhibition visitors. I have enjoyed working on this project as I have great expectations for young designers, and I like transferring my experience and enthusiasm to them.

Through your work you link education with industry and industry with the public. Do you think there is a common language of design?

The language of design is starting to be understood by a broader audience, thanks to fashion blogs, fashion shows on the internet and e-commerce. It's mainly the language for younger consumers who have easy access to new communication technologies.

What upcoming trends have you noticed in yarn and knitting?

New trends for yarn and knitting involve research into quality, investing in multiblends of natural fibres, playing with random-dyed, pre-dyed, multiple melange and colour effects.

Fancy yarns are still strongly influenced by nature, sometimes with a primordial look, but lightweight, soft and voluminous. Shiny metallic, reflective sparkles are still very important. Oxidized metallic effects often accompany rough natural yarns.

Knits are assuming wide, comfortable proportions, and investment pieces can be any type of garment, from bold knitted coats to slimmer dresses to accessories. Three-dimensional relief stitches are also very much on-trend.

What's next for you?

I am organizing a Knitwear Master Course in our knitting laboratory, in association with the Politecnico in Milan, to enable FIT students to expand their knowledge of innovative technologies in order to promote their creative ideas.

19.

Happy End Is A Matter Of Faith • Hesperia • Spring-Summer 2015
TEXTILES
Metronomy
Psychic
Random
FASH
Spring-Summer
The Memories for You
power you have.
intercolor

1

2

3

4

1. Trend-development work in progress for Intercolor, Paris, June 2013.

2, 3, 4. Design sketches by Elementi Moda for men's and women's garments.

5

5. Xiao Li of the Royal College of Art, London, winner of the 2012 Feel the Yarn exhibition organised by Ornella Bignami each year at the Pitti Filati trade show. The exhibition pairs student knitwear designers with top professionals in the Italian spinning industry.

6. Yiyi Guo, winner of Feel the Yarn 2013, with her designs.

23.

.38
Yiyi Guo
.39
Yiyi Guo
北京服装学院
BEIJING INSTITUTE OF FASHION TECHNOLOGY

6

7

8

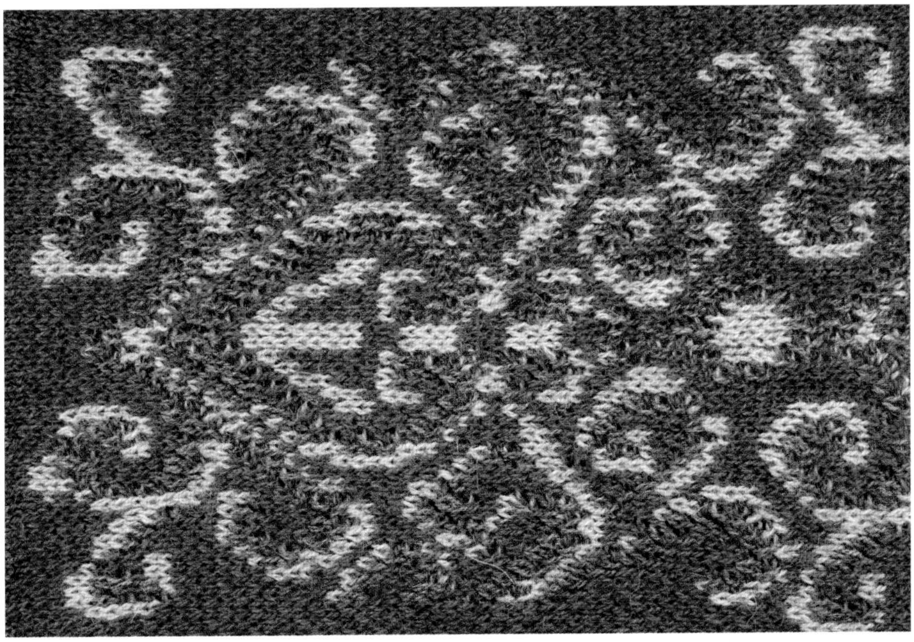

9

7, 8, 9. Knit swatches demonstrating stitches developed by Elementi Moda for Italian yarn manufacturer Alpes. Bignami calls these 'Structures'.

Mark Fast

Canadian Mark Fast graduated from London's Central Saint Martins in 2008, and he has since engaged in numerous collaborations with designers including Stuart Vevers (for Loewe), Bora Aksu, Christian Louboutin, Swarovski and Atelier Swarovski, Topshop, Pinko, Danier (leather goods) and Woolmark.

Mark's unmistakable womenswear pieces, which are created on a domestic knitting machine, have challenged perceptions of knitted garments. He is famous for devising his own innovative stitches, and embracing stretch yarns to create contemporary sculptured garments. His pieces have a unique design signature and a large following. A champion for women (having famously sent a plus-size model down a London catwalk in 2010 to prove that his knitwear could look good on any woman), Mark takes pleasure in the joy he creates with his garments.

How would you describe your work? Who buys your label?

My work is a mix of so many things. Engineering techniques from my machine over the body. It's a calculation of madness. My work also has a cinematic quality, being inspired by different characters from movies or in my mind.

Those who buy from my label are really aware of the number of hours and detailing that go into my pieces. They are purchasing a piece of long-lasting craftsmanship.

What keeps you designing knit?

Knitwear is a challenge for me and it keeps my mind in check with my soul. It gives me a way to express myself. With knitwear it is also a form of control. From the thread to the end dress, I am in control. When a woman is happy and feels sexy and beautiful in one of my creations, I am happy. It is this daily quest for something to enhance a person's life that keeps me going.

What is a typical day's work for you?

I am always working – during the day, in the night, and mostly in my dreams. It does not switch off for me.

Can you explain how you decide on each season's concept?

It comes from a trip, or a movie I've watched, where I want to replay the feeling and experience I had. Concepts are quite emotional for me. This is how I use my collections. They become intricately therapeutic.

Can you describe your creative thinking process, and how this is realized as products?

It starts with research and music and cinema. I am sensitive to my surroundings and pick up ideas from travelling to being in a concentrated orb of inspiration. This moves into my knitwear, where I want to create that same kind of excitement. There is so much experimenting, draping, shouting and throwing before an idea comes into a peaceful chaos.

Your pieces have a strong identity, with an emphasis on stitch detail and construction. At what stage of the design process do you consider materials and technologies?

I always start with the yarn and mould it into the creations in my head. The most important part of the design process is the fit and the fabric. Once you've got this down, you have a happy beauty.

Hand knit or machine knit?

I like a mixture of both. In my last show I used crochet and machine knit. Machine-knitting is misunderstood, because it is someone in control of the machine. This is still a handmade process! I find the machines to be quite obscure inventions that I am still getting my head around. Very inspiring.

Who has inspired you the most?

My parents. My dad is the most inspiring man I know; he is such a good man and has been such a big support in my career. My mother has never missed a show and has always been accepting of how I express myself.

What do you consider to be the greatest challenge facing knitwear designers at present?

The lack of exciting yarn! We have to reinvent our own ideas as we knit in order to find and create something new. This challenge, however, brings thrilling creativity and innovation. Maybe we should leave it this way!

How do you see the Mark Fast label developing?

I see it moving into different collaborations with design and architecture. Menswear is a thought, and I also want to push my diffusion line 'Faster' into its next context.

I would also love to keep working in India in a major way. I love it there – the people, the colour, the intensity. It is fascinating.

27.

1

2

3

1. Orange and pink zigzag knit dress and scarf, reworking a twinset idea.

2. Blue and black dress and chunky scarf.

3. Red dress with fringe detail caught into the knitted fabric.

4. Autumn/winter designs at London Fashion Week showcasing a range of techniques.

29.

4

Fashion: Mark Fast

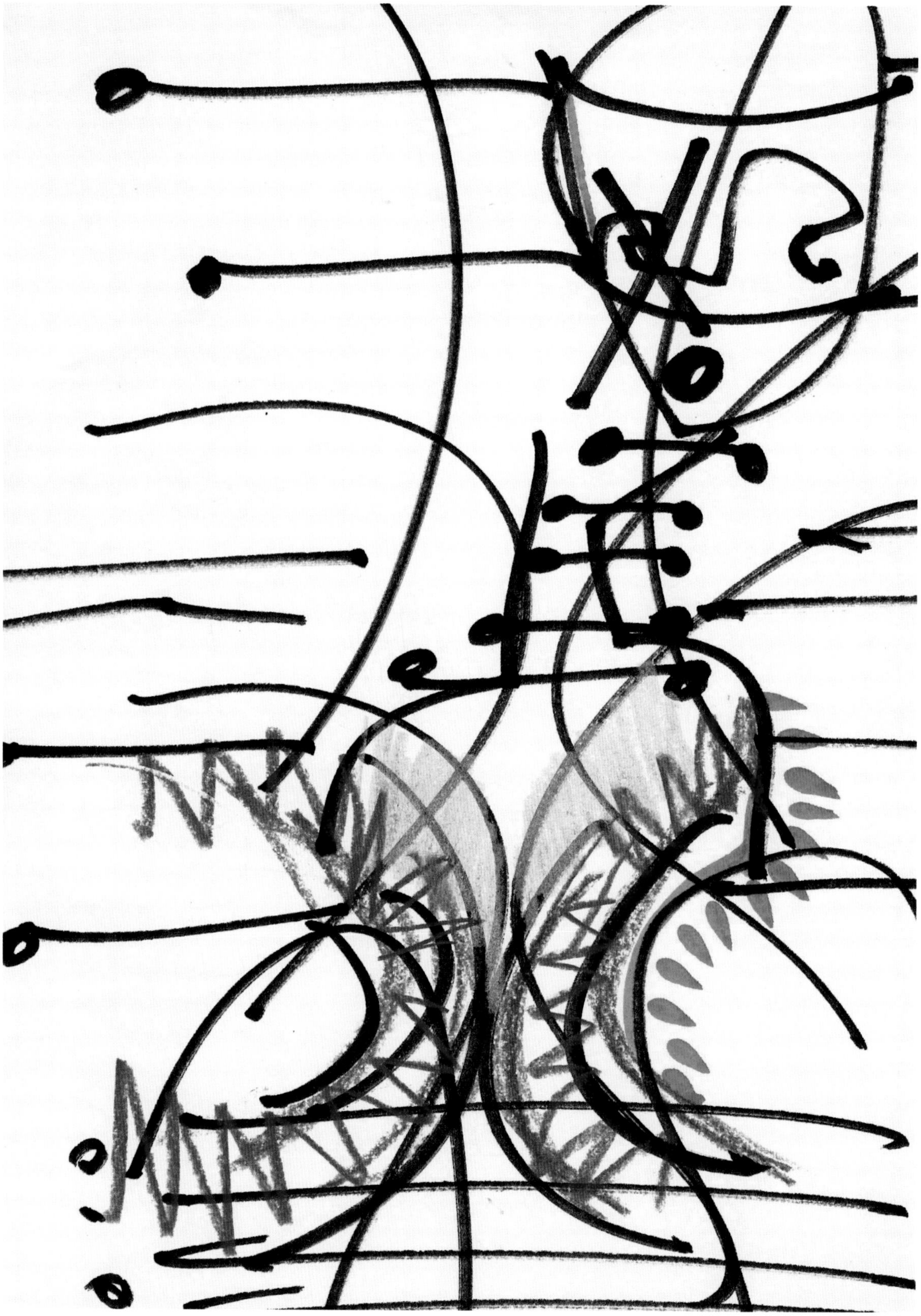

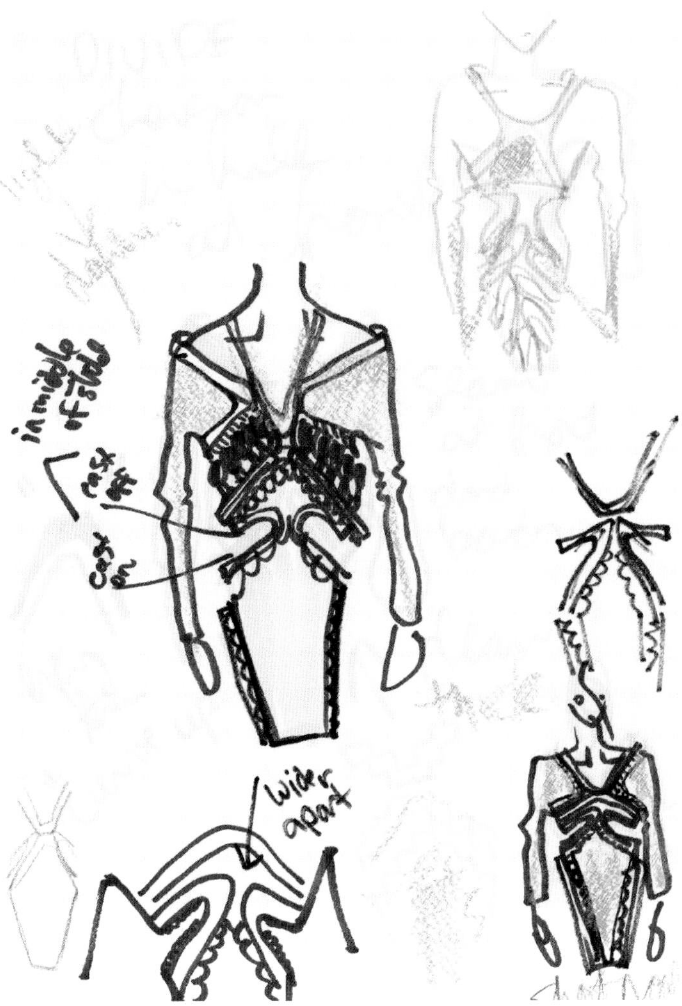

6

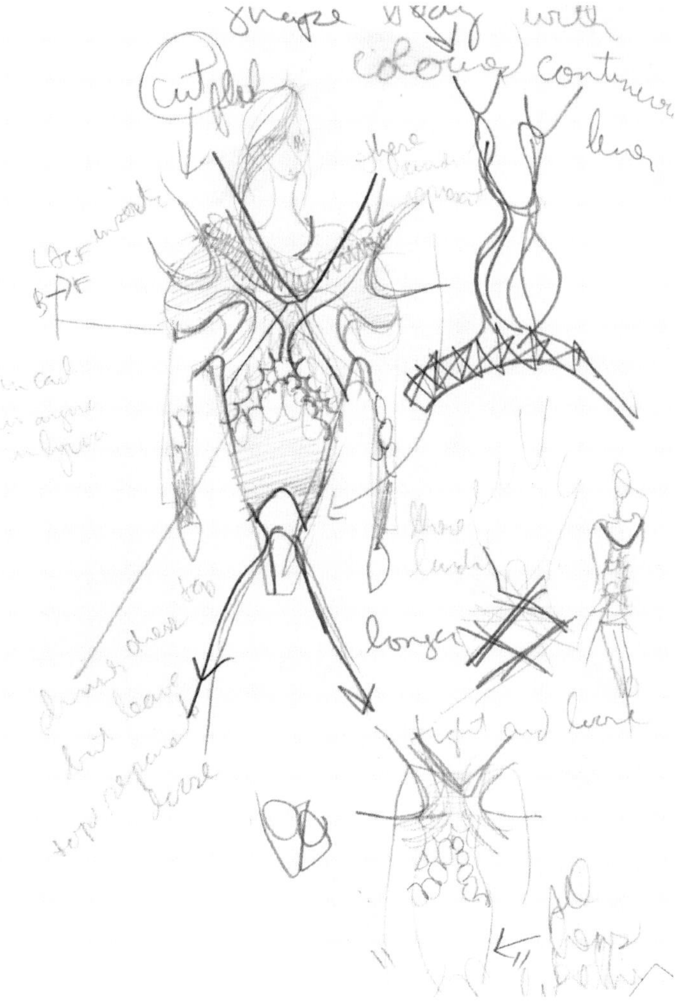

7

5, 6, 7. Design sketches.

8

9

8. This spring/summer black and grey dress with fringes is a classic Mark Fast look, enhancing the silhouette.

9. Singer Beyoncé onstage in Central Park, New York, in a lacy yellow Mark Fast knit dress.

Ramón Gurillo

Ramón Gurillo is a fashion designer from Valencia, Spain. He gained his knowledge of the fashion industry by working as a model booker before relocating to London in the 1990s and launching his label. Inspired by his surroundings, Gurillo's influences are multicultural: traditional Valencian craftsmanship combined with a London sensibility and a 'hint of rock 'n' roll'.

Gurillo's intricate designs, with recurring open-weave stitches, often cocoon-like in silhouette, use the finest yarns, refined cottons, linens and crêpes. His collections were sold to Liberty department store in 2001 and are now stocked in other iconic London stores, such as Browns. He was also a finalist at the 2007 UK Fashion Export Awards.

Gurillo's beautifully wearable collections are currently available in the UK, Japan, America, Italy, Spain and France, and he presents catwalk shows in London, Paris, New York and India.

How would you describe your work? Who buys your label?

Handcrafted knits using high-quality yarns and true artisan skills, with a Mediterranean heritage and a cosmopolitan outlook. Our clients are men and women who have confidence in their style.

What keeps you designing knit?

There are so many possibilities in the tradition of knitwear. We are a very creative team, working to develop new ideas, and this is very exciting.

What is your role within the company?

I am the creative director of the label; my job is to build the collections, putting together the ideas and bringing together the team's skills. I keep the knitters interested, and always looking forward to new challenges.

Can you explain how you decide on each season's concept?

At the start of the season, I put together mood boards to create the atmosphere of the collection. Our creative decisions then refer back to that, but we are always open-minded during development.

How would you describe the design aesthetic behind Ramón Gurillo?

I would say Valencian craftsmanship has been modernized, by taking inspiration from London's vibe along with a hint of rock 'n' roll. Travelling also inspires me.

Your pieces seem to reflect your environment, with an emphasis on yarn choice and stitch. At what stage of the design process do you consider materials and technologies?

Materials and the way to execute the garments are so important – from the very start of the process. Finest natural fibres – merino wool, alpaca, cottons, linens, silks – are always the base of our collections. Our knitters are true artisans with so much knowledge, and this really helps to develop my designs.

Hand knit or machine knit?

We have specialized in hand-knitting since the beginning. Both techniques have different outcomes. We use both and can produce very interesting results.

Where is your production done?

Our production is done in Valencia and surrounding villages, where there is a great tradition of hand-knitting. My team have a lifetime of knitting experience. We work on keeping this tradition going.

Who has inspired you the most?

I like the work of Dries Van Noten, Alber Elbaz for Lanvin, and Japanese designers such as Yamamoto and Comme des Garçons. But my biggest inspiration is the late Spanish designer Jesús del Pozo, whose work was brilliant.

How do you see the Ramón Gurillo label developing?

I want to grow the business across the men's and women's ranges (lines). We are also looking seriously at an online shop.

35.

1

2

1. Red knit lace dress from Ramón Gurillo's ready-to-wear collection.

2. Knit features heavily in Gurillo's ready-to-wear collections, showcased here on the catwalk in Valencia, Spain.

3. Chunky knits from Gurillo's menswear collection. Gurillo's attention to detail is evident in the use of the purl stitch on the cuff to create a hem.

Fashion: Ramón Gurillo

4

5

4. Gurillo has cleverly left the ends of the yarn unfinished to create tassels, enhancing the boxy shape of this poncho dress.

5. This textured, gathered knit dress features a ruffled effect.

6

6. Off-the-shoulder, loosely woven knit dress.

7. The exaggerated stitch in this open-knit dress adds interest to the simple shift shape.

41.

7

John Smedley

John Smedley was founded in the Derbyshire village of Lea Mills by John Smedley and Peter Nightingale in 1784. The site was chosen for its brook, which provided water to clean the yarn and power the mill; it is now a World Heritage Site. Still operating out of the same buildings, John Smedley is perhaps the world's longest-running factory and manufacturer.

Ian Maclean (seventh generation of this family business) is the current managing director, responsible for leading the company into the twenty-first century. John Smedley's quality garments are made in the UK and exported to over 70 countries.

Collaboration has been very successful for John Smedley. How do you decide who to work with?

Collaborations can come from anywhere, but we are always choosy as to who we work with, and what the outcome will be – it has to be enhancing for both brands to be worthwhile.

Vivienne Westwood is originally from Derbyshire. We requested her participation in a collaboration in the 1990s and she provided us with a series of sketches that we were able to interpret into garments.

Junya Watanabe (Comme des Garçons) collaborated with us for his MAN line for several seasons; the way he likes to work is very particular: he selects two or three styles he likes, and he will then overdye the garments in different shades of blue, so that the seams remain in the contrasting white. A subtle detail, but very much of his own brand vision, which was then combined with John Smedley quality.

Umbro, the British sportswear brand, approached us in the run-up to the London 2012 Olympics. They had made the original 1948 Olympic team kits, including sports shirts, vests (tank tops), shorts and track tops. They wanted to recreate these old garments, but with a modern twist.

How do you showcase the work you do?

We are still a wholesale business at the core, and our selling tools are quite conventional – the sales presenter, colour card, look book, etc. The UK is still our biggest market and we showcase our products at trade events in London.

We have had a transactional website since 1998 – we were early in the game! This enables a very small brand like ourselves to project brand values and imagery to a global audience at a relatively low cost. The website is now as a key media channel for expressing our brand, and probably our most important showcase. We have complete control over it, so it really is our story, the way we want to tell it.

John Smedley has consistently embraced technology, from water-powered mills to state-of-the-art electronic equipment. Will this continue, and are there any methods that transcend time?

John Smedley has always gone its own way, almost to the extent of developing its own technologies. This obviously adds cost, but it does make for interesting discussions about how to develop in the future.

Investments in technology are becoming more expensive as machines are driven by ever more complex software. The skills required to program the software are also in short supply and therefore costly. We continue to invest in all of these areas – sometimes experimentally – to stay ahead of the developments.

A key issue at present is the concept of seamless garments, manufactured on Shima Seiki WholeGarment machines. A feature of the 30gg John Smedley garment is its soft, linked seams, resulting from traditional fully fashioned manufacturing. While there are obvious advantages to using WholeGarment, we have no idea how much the seams mean to our consumers. It is possible that this feature of our garments may transcend time (and technological advances!).

What would you say has been the greatest innovation in knit in the last 100 years?

The idea that a brand can be worth more than a garment. This has revolutionized volume knitwear, raising margins and the potential to advertise.

Do you encourage a close relationship between technicians and designers at John Smedley?

For those who develop the software used to program modern knitting machines, the designer and the technician are one person. While this may be the case in the product-development team at the knitting-machine manufacturer, in the real world the two skills are still very much separate! I am yet to meet the perfect designer/technician.

How do you see the John Smedley label developing?

I want to significantly enhance the John Smedley brand and grow its capital value hugely. The history of John Smedley is, in effect, the history of manufacturing. I would like to see us build a great British brand that, at its core, gives the lie to the notion that we don't have a future for manufacturing in the UK. I want to leave John Smedley in a healthier state than I found it, employing far more people in the UK and projecting our brand values around the world. In this sense, I am both a contrarian and ambitious for my family's company, so watch this space.

1

2

3

4

1. A contemporary John Smedley shop front.

2. Historical photo of workers winding yarn in the John Smedley factory.

3, 4. John Smedley women's knitwear designs from the 1930s – a golfing dress and nightwear – showcasing careful construction and quality of finish that John Smedley is known for.

5

6

5, 6, 7. Contemporary John Smedley men's knitwear: the Parallel sweater, the Kelby sweater, and the Richards roll-neck pullover.

Fashion: John Smedley

7

Fashion: John Smedley

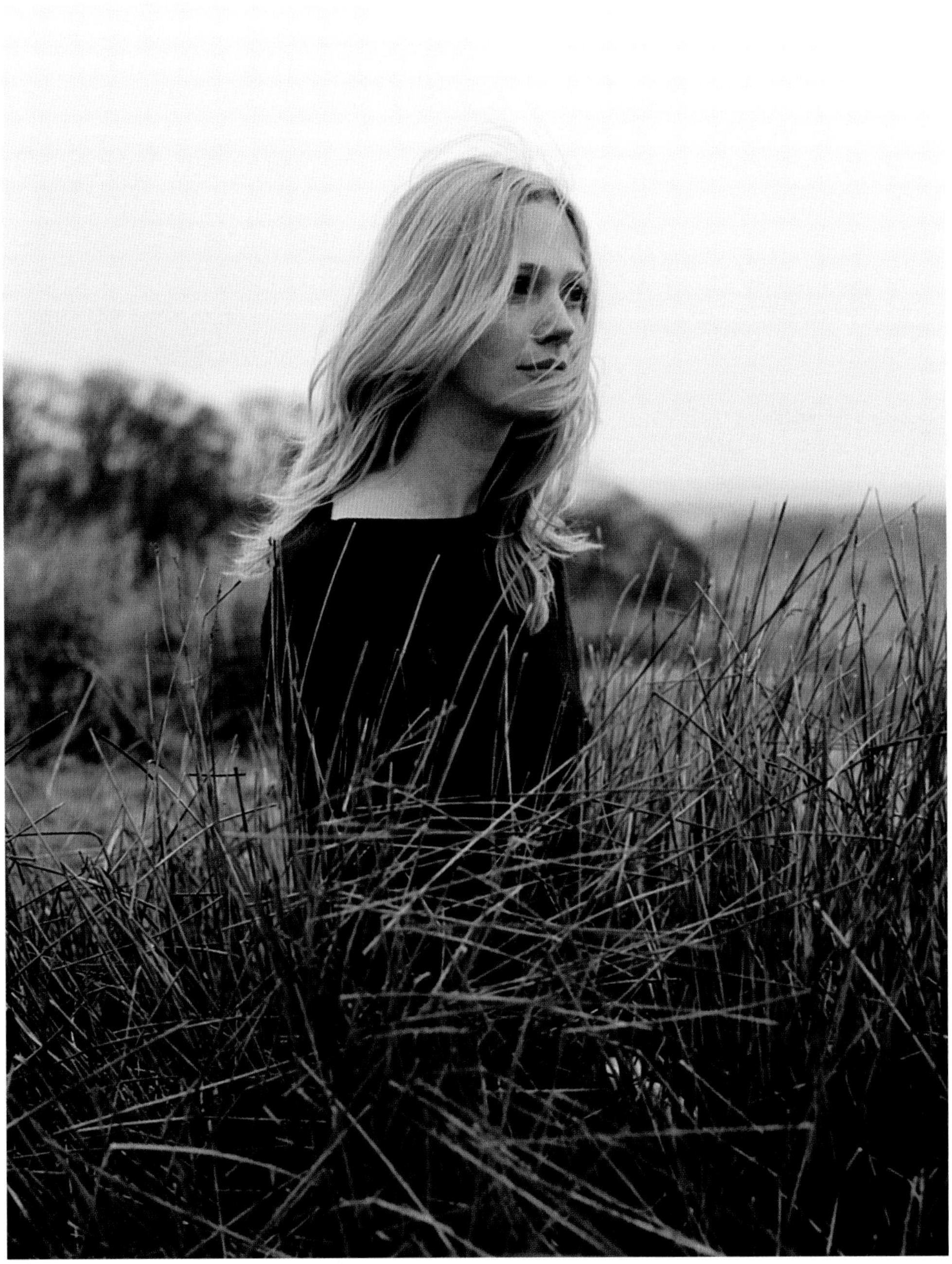

9

10

8, 9, 10. Contemporary John Smedley women's knitwear: the classic boat-neck Susan sweater, the Cassandra sweater, and the Malachy short-sleeved sweater. These classic styles are knitted with the finest merino wool and finished by hand.

Leutton Postle

London-based luxury knitwear label Leutton Postle was set up by long-time friends and collaborators Sam Leutton and Jenny Postle (the pair met on their BA course at London's Central Saint Martins in 2005). Their label draws on a range of influences to create wearable, craft-led collections that are not limited by trends. Their design approach freely embraces colour, unusual surface texture and rich patterns to create beautifully offbeat knits for women. Leutton Postle represents a labour of love and a shared creative vision, which can be seen in the extraordinary attention to detail in each garment.

Launching at London Fashion Week in September 2011, their work was then showcased by Fashion Scout after winning their much-coveted Merit Award for Spring/Summer 2012. For London Fashion Week 2014, the label showcased their first film at Somerset House, as part of the British Fashion Council's Fash/On Film initiative, and also exhibited in the BFC's Designer Showrooms.

What are your roles within the company?

Jenny and I [Sam Leutton] have similar backgrounds in textiles and knit. We research and design separately, then discuss and hash out our ideas together. In between designing collections, we have different roles within the company. There are three of us in total – myself, Jenny and Louise Welsh. I focus on production, Jenny is responsible for a lot of our social media and marketing, and Louise manages sales and administration, although these roles are blurred; we all do a bit of everything.

How do you decide each season's concept?

We're not hugely into concepts – for us it is very much about the visual content of a collection. We pick a few areas to research, but often our biggest inspirations come not from certain themes but from select imagery that we come across in our day-to-day lives. We then collate all this research and begin to edit it down, which results in an overall idea.

How would you describe the design philosophy behind Leutton Postle?

We don't take ourselves too seriously, and we like to think this is evident in our collections. We're quite jokey, daft, vibrant people.

How do you select fabrics? Can you describe your creative thinking process and how this is realized as products?

We use mostly machine-knitted fabrics, made on Stoll machines. We basically take all our research up to our sampling centre in Leicester and sit down with a technician and try out a few different ideas. We used to spend ages doing this, but now we have less time so we do about a day or two of sampling and testing out these ideas and our chosen yarns.

Once we have an idea of the knits we are going to use, we draw from our shape research and start draping and testing out the fabrics on the body. Then it all becomes a bit of a whirlwind of toileing (creating muslins), sampling and testing finishings. We have a very freestyle approach to designing really. We probably should be a bit more organized.

Do you collaborate at all?

We mostly collaborate with stylists for certain shoots. Notably we were commissioned by *Garage* magazine to make five sweaters with written manifestos emblazoned on them.

Any other projects you are working on?

We are doing some sweaters for a non-fashion brand, and we have a few other projects in the pipeline. A lot of the time we can't discuss such projects fully until they are set in stone.

At what stage of the design process do you consider materials and technologies?

Right from the beginning. The yarn, the colour, the fabrics and how we make them are quite crucial to us. All the fabrics we use are made by us or especially for us, so it is very important that these are strong and speak our aesthetic. With regards to technology, we use computerized knitting machines to ensure our fabrics are commercially viable whilst still being visually exciting.

Colour and pattern are fundamental to your brand. How do you research these?

We research what we like visually and this is quite constant. I'm forever saving images and cut-outs, taking photos and researching. It's important for us to have a lot of things to take inspiration from.

Which stitches and yarns do you favour?

We make a lot of jacquard fabrics mixed with domestic knits, using a variety of yarns. We use a lot of Lurex because they have such a great range of bright, iridescent yarns in many different colours. They also knit really well. We like to add in some weird yarns, which add a different texture. We'll choose one or two fancy yarns to stop everything looking too flat, which is a risk with knitted jacquards.

How do you see the Leutton Postle label developing?

We want to continue to make wearable, visually exciting, atypical knitwear. We aim to expand our list of stockists and grow steadily as a label, and to become renowned for our unusual mix of colour and texture.

51.

1

52.

3

1. An overprinted pleated knit skirt is teamed with a jacquard sweater in this autumn/winter ensemble.

2, 3. Print and knit techniques are brought together to create original fashion pieces showcasing Leutton Postle's unique style.

4

4. Pattern is used expertly to create contrast in this spring/summer asymmetric skirt.

5. Note the craft detail added to the hems of the top and skirt, updating macramé and crochet.

55.

56.

7

6. Texture and technique sit together beautifully in this sheer spring/summer dress.

7. Here knit is used to create striking vertical, rather than horizontal, stripes.

Markus Lupfer

Markus Lupfer is a graduate of London's Westminster University, and an award-winning designer (a recipient of the British Fashion Council's Newgen scheme, and Best Designer of the Year at the Prix de la Mode Awards in Spain). He has worked for established fashion houses including Cacharel, Mulberry and Armand Basi, where he was Design Director. Markus now shows at London Fashion Week under his own-name label.

Markus Lupfer knitwear is renowned for its high quality and beautiful finish; the label has a large celebrity following, and pieces are often featured in editorials and on screen. Markus is particularly famous for his humorous and subversive embellished sweaters.

What is your role within the company?

I am the owner and creative director of the Markus Lupfer brand. I oversee both the womenswear and menswear collections, and the shoe ranges (lines) too. I am very involved with all aspects of the business and really enjoy the whole process.

Can you explain how you decide on each season's concept?

Each season begins with an instinct for an idea, something that really excites me at that time, so we build up mood boards and then start to focus in on certain ideas and themes, and it develops from there into the final collection.

How would you describe the design philosophy behind Markus Lupfer?

The Markus Lupfer customer is someone who wants to look amazing and gorgeous in special pieces, but still knows how to have fun. We always try to keep this element, whether it's a tongue-in-cheek slogan on a T-shirt, or a sequinned animal on a knitted sweater. We want her to put on a Markus Lupfer piece and smile, so I always have this in mind from the beginning. If it makes us smile in the studio then we are usually on to a good thing!

Your pieces are a favourite with celebrities. Have you designed anything specifically for a personality, and does the process differ from your normal way of working?

We have designed some exciting pieces for some special celebrities. These pieces are ordinarily developed using the same formalities as our other samples. Of course, these pieces often need to be made to deadlines, so they tend to have shorter timescales to work to. We therefore usually produce them in-house and we liaise very closely with the client and their stylist.

At what stage of the design process do you consider materials and technologies?

Choosing the yarns and yarn colours is always the first stage of a new season, so it's a very crucial part. The technology of knitwear is really important, and exploring new techniques that we can develop through our knitwear is always very exciting.

You are known for your iconic embellished sweaters. How do you see this developing?

Everybody still loves our sequin sweaters, they are a big favourite, but we are constantly researching and offering new techniques through the knitwear. Intarsia, new embroidery methods and other embellishments are just some of them. We like to push things forward constantly whilst remaining true to the elements that have allowed the business to get to where it is today.

Who has inspired you the most?

I really admire artists like Jeff Koons and Keith Haring, who create (or created) such inspiring works and managed to inject humour and fun into their work whilst still being taken seriously in their field.

How do you see the Markus Lupfer label developing?

The label is expanding all the time. We have recently launched shoes under the Markus Lupfer label and are looking more towards our accessories and extending our offerings in all of aspects of our ready to wear. The brand is at a very exciting stage – there is always a lot going on, and that's how I like it!

59.

1

2

3

1. This embellished motif sweater, twinned with a woven jacquard trouser, demonstrates the signature clean silhouette that Markus has developed. The collection it comes from was inspired by artists such as Sonia Delaunay, Mark Rothko and Jean-Michel Basquiat.

2, 3. Both top and trouser here are made from merino wool, with a striking allover snakeskin print.

4. This crown-embellished sweater was inspired by Basquiat.

4

5

5. This line-up sketch demonstrates clean lines and silhouettes. Note, too, how the placement of detail has been distributed evenly throughout the collection.

Fashion: Markus Lupfer

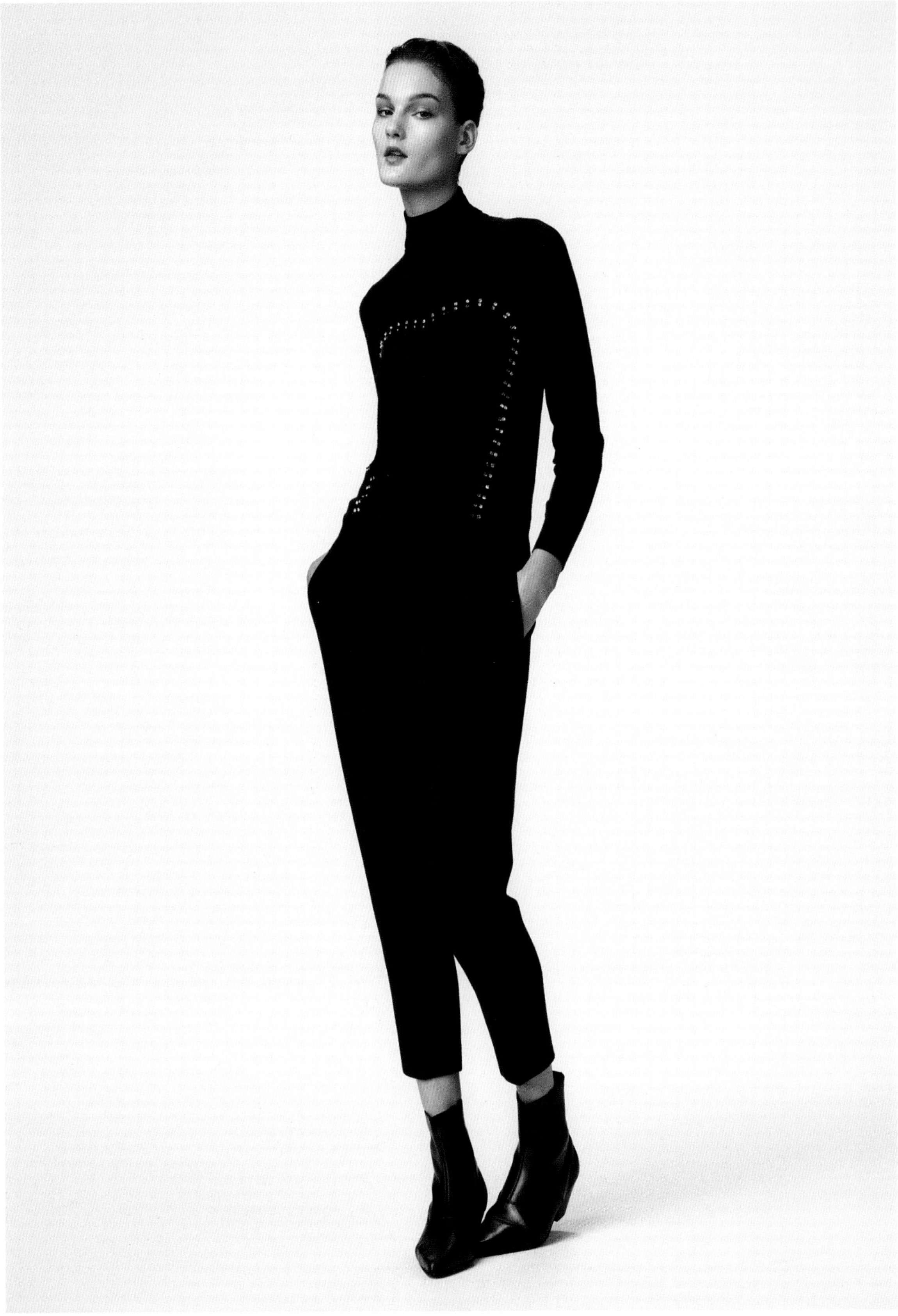

6

7

6. This merino wool polo-neck sweater features an intarsia front bodice panel detail, finished with a jewel embellishment.

7. The jacquard in this piece has been broken up by clever use of panels and varied with contrasting scale and pattern.

Irina Shaposhnikova

Irina Shaposhnikova began her career studying fashion design at the London College of Fashion. One year later, she moved to Antwerp, continuing her studies at the Antwerp Royal Academy of Fine Arts. After that, she continued working in her studio in Antwerp, also taking part in various exhibitions and projects around the world. She is currently working in collaboration with a Moscow-based production company as a designer and pattern maker, as well as teaching at the British Higher School of Art and Design, also in Moscow.

Can you explain how you decide on a concept?

Usually I start with the idea of what I want to do and then begin doing the research, fabric samples, etc. I like to experiment with materials and develop new techniques; sometimes during the process I come up with another idea that I want to develop further, but usually I try to stay focused. The concept is a starting point for me, but then it might transform into something different.

Are you affected by your environment? Where do you now live?

I am living between Moscow and Antwerp at the moment. I guess the fact that I come from Russia and lived in Europe for several years has affected me both as a person and as a designer. But studying at the Antwerp Academy, which is a very international school, has also influenced my work a lot.

Can you describe your creative thinking process, and how this is realized as products?

I try to create pieces that are simultaneously innovative, modern and timeless. Therefore I experiment a lot and work on developing new techniques and materials. This is an essential part of the design process for me. I don't really follow trends; instead, I try to create pieces that are more couture and unique.

You use interesting combinations of yarn to create surface interest and structure. Why do you choose to use knit to interpret these ideas? What other materials do you use?

I wanted to create something that is both very light and structured. I was interested in hand knits and wanted to make them look more modern, so I started experimenting with various types of knits and combining them together. As a result, I have created several pieces that are made of knitted cables sewn on to transparent mesh in combination with elements of the traditional sweater.

For my 'Crystallographica' collection I experimented with plastics, combining them with woven fabrics such as silk organza, wool and light-reflecting textiles.

At what stage of the design process do you consider materials and technologies?

I think technologies are very important nowadays, especially when it comes to textile development or knitwear, because they give new possibilities to designers. For example, with the development of 3D printing it became possible to print ready-made garments and customize them. And designers like Iris van Herpen are pushing the boundaries of rapid prototyping, creating garments made of flexible 3D-printed materials. I believe that intersection of design and technology will be the future of fashion. As a designer, I think there is always going to be an appreciation of handcraft, but it is interesting to see how it might be influenced by technology.

Which stitches and yarns do you favour?

I like to work with wool.

Where are your collections stocked? Where do your pieces reside?

The studio is based in Antwerp, but I travel between Moscow and Antwerp, and some things are being produced in Russia too. For the moment, I mostly work with custom-made pieces and private clients.

Have you collaborated with any other designers/artists?

I have collaborated with the Antwerp-based jewellery designer Heaven Tanudiredja, who created beautiful jewellery pieces for my collection. I have also collaborated with the visual artist Pierre Debusschere, who made a short film for me.

Who has inspired you the most?

Nicolas Ghesquière [creative director of Louis Vuitton] is one of the designers I admire the most, also Miuccia Prada.

How do you see your work developing?

It is very important for me to stay creative in anything I do. In the future I plan to develop a new collection and expand my brand.

1

2

1. Irina's 'Crystallographica' collection combines woven fabrics with plastics, and showcases her skill as a pattern cutter.

2, 3. Applied three-dimensional cables on a sheer monofilament knit create a stunning piece of knitwear.

69.

3

4

5

4. Here Irina has created jewellery from exaggerated knitted tubes.

5. A monofilament knit acts as the base for chunky cables and oversized sweater details such as a roll neck and ribbed cuffs and hem.

6

7

6, 7. The use of gold yarn in these signature pieces gives the knitwear an ecclesiastical feel.

Shima Seiki

Shima Seiki was established as a business by Masahiro Shima in 1962. During the half-century that it has been trading, the company has become a world leader in the manufacture, development, sales and marketing of computerized knitting machines and software systems. Shima Seiki introduced whole-garment knitting technology to the industry, enabling designers to realize knitted garments without seams, a development that continues to revolutionize knitwear. The company now has a global sales network spanning more than 80 countries, including all major knit-manufacturing markets around the world. Masaki Karasuno of Shima Seiki speaks to us about the company.

How does it work in your company – do designers come to you with ideas, or do you present to them?

Shima Seiki regularly produces knitwear samples for customer reference in order to maximize the effectiveness of their knitting machines. We produce 50 to 100 samples per month and upload them to our users' site, where registered members can download programming data for their own use. In addition, we also accept orders for engineering specialty designs.

How do you showcase the work you do?

We publish look books showcasing our samples twice a year. We also have samples on display at our design centres in Tokyo, Osaka, Hong Kong, Shanghai, New York and Milan. Samples are also shown at trade exhibitions and private shows, and the occasional fashion show.

What gauge machines can you use?

Our machines range from 3G to 21G, and because of our 'WideGauge' variable-gauge technology, knitwear produced on our machines can have fabric texture ranging from 2G to 26G, which is the widest range possible on computerized flat-knitting machinery.

How do you predict trends?

We research colour and stitch trends using resources like pre-season projections, and also information from Première Vision, Pitti Filati, and various colour and trend seminars. We also have an in-house colour specialist.

Would you say design is driven by technology?

Having had the honorable position of leading the industry down the path of technological innovation for some time now, Shima Seiki can say with confidence that most of the design breakthroughs seen in knit fashion have only become possible with technical innovations that permit such breakthroughs. An example is our WholeGarment technology, which allows designs to wrap around the entire body without interruption from seams.

Technicians come to you to learn how to use the machines. Do you also train designers?

Our product line covers the entire supply chain for knitting as well as for other fashion-related industries. We offer training programmes for each product. Knit technicians enter our training programme to learn how to use knitting machines. Designers and patterners also come to learn how to use our design systems; they can also take courses in knit programming and knitting in order to have a better understanding of how their designs are realized as products.

Do you have any programmes to encourage young designers to embrace new technology?

Your concern for young designers is a valid point in that the younger generation is consistently losing interest in textiles, as can be seen from the emigration of young labour forces away from textile-related occupations. That is why it is important to promote knitting with high technological content. We contribute, to varying degrees, to educational facilities in order to provide hands-on experience to budding knitting technologists.

What would you say has been the greatest innovation in knit in the last ten years?

Like many other industries, the production of knits and other textiles in the twentieth century was marked by great advancements in machine technology and computerization. By contrast, the new millennium has seen significant improvements in software.

What do you predict for knit in the future?

We have already invented the future of knitting – WholeGarment. We said this back in 1995, when we released it to a bedazzled but sceptical audience who wondered if the technology was something before its time. Indeed it was, because WholeGarment was launched five years prior to its original plan, in order to help protect the Japanese knitting industry against cheap imports.

Nearly 20 years on, WholeGarment has seen great advancements in its capabilities and its proliferation, becoming the primary knit production method for many customers. Currently WholeGarment knitting machines account for approximately 5 per cent of the total number of machines sold at Shima Seiki, and that number is rising yearly.

1

2

3

1

1. A Shima Seiki design on the catwalk during the 3rd Knitwear Designers Contest at the A/W13 Hong Kong Fashion Week.

2. Contrast is a key feature of this design, accentuated by the use of different yarns.

3. This dress showcases partial/hold knitting – a machine-knitting technique in which only part of a row is knitted – for a striking textural effect.

4

4. Bright and playful Shima Seiki children's designs on the catwalk during the Knitwear Innovation and Design Society show at the A/W13 Hong Kong Fashion Week.

5, 6. Swatches demonstrating the variety of textured stitches that Shima Seiki machines can work. Shima Seiki research colour and stitch trends carefully and produce a range of knitwear samples for their customers.

5

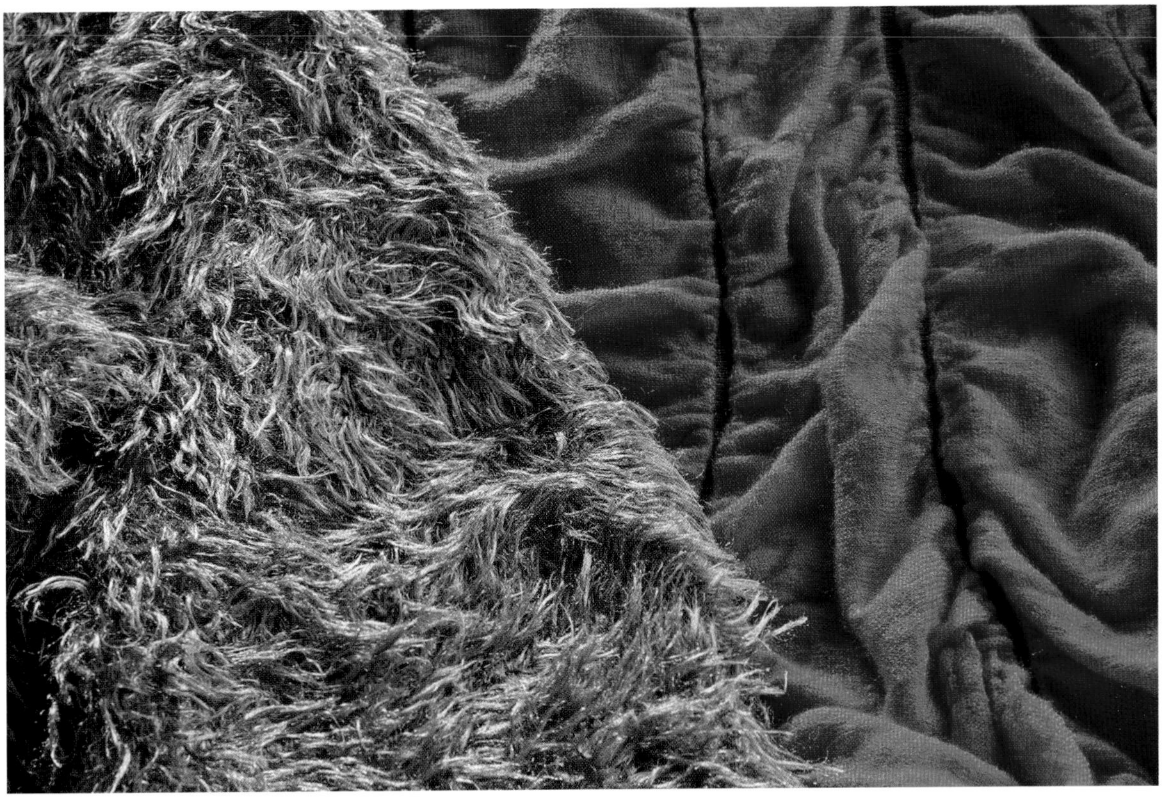

6

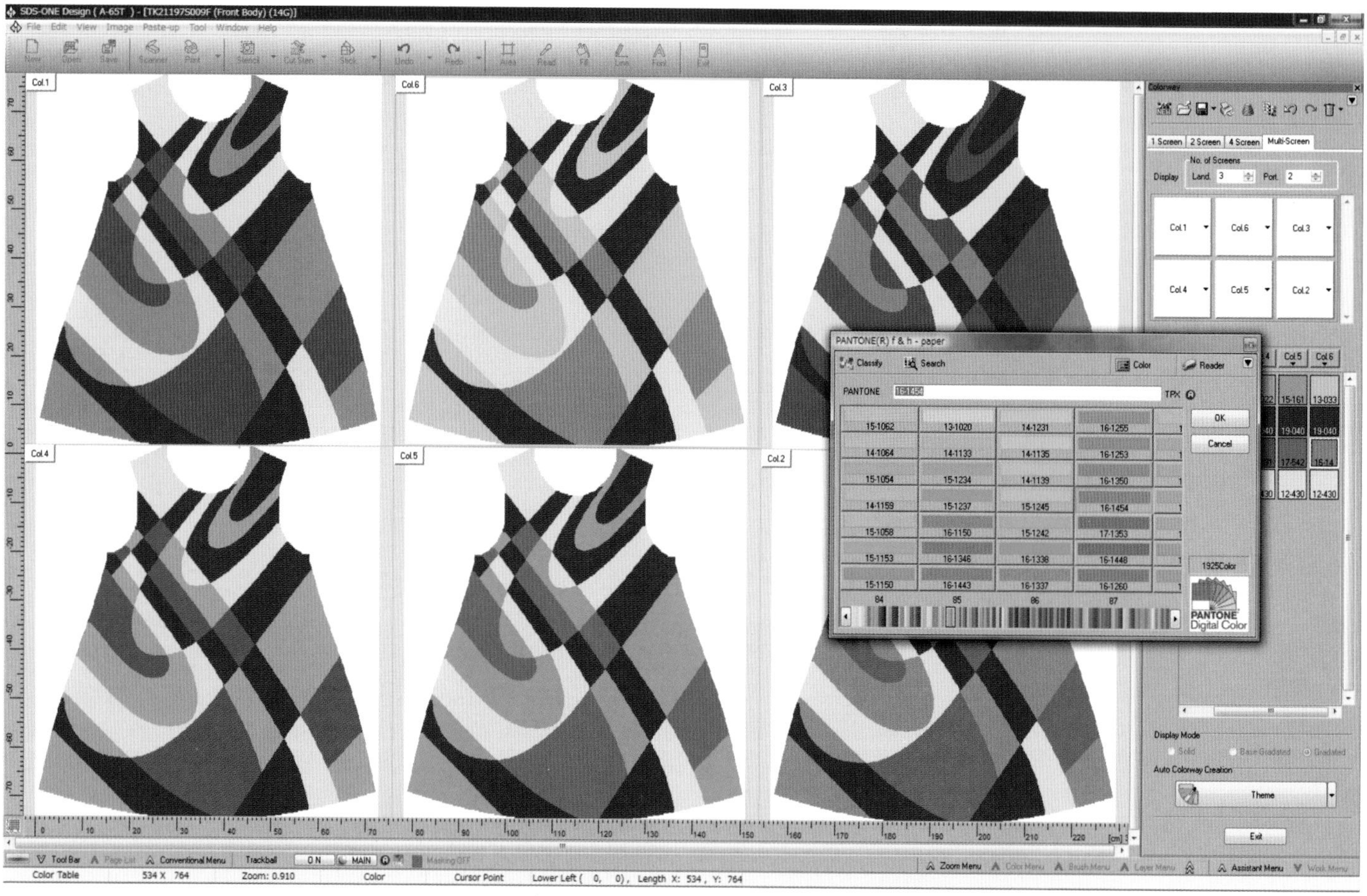
SDS-ONE Design (A-65T) - [TK21197S009F (Front Body) (14G)]
Col.1
Col.6
Col.3
Col.4
Col.5
Col.2
Colorway
1 Screen
2 Screen
4 Screen
Multi-Screen
No. of Screens
Display
Land.
Port.
PANTONE(R) f & h - paper
Classify
Search
Color
Reader
PANTONE
TPX
OK
Cancel
15-1062
13-1020
14-1231
16-1255
14-1064
14-1133
14-1135
16-1253
15-1054
15-1234
14-1139
16-1350
14-1159
15-1237
15-1245
16-1454
15-1058
16-1150
15-1242
17-1353
15-1153
16-1346
16-1338
16-1448
15-1150
16-1443
16-1337
16-1260
84
85
86
87
1925Color
PANTONE
Digital Color
Display Mode
Auto Colorway Creation
Theme
Exit
Tool Bar
Conventional Menu
Trackball
ON
MAIN
Color Table
534 X 764
Zoom: 0.910
Color
Cursor Point
Lower Left (0, 0), Length X: 534 , Y: 764
Zoom Menu
Assistant Menu

7

8

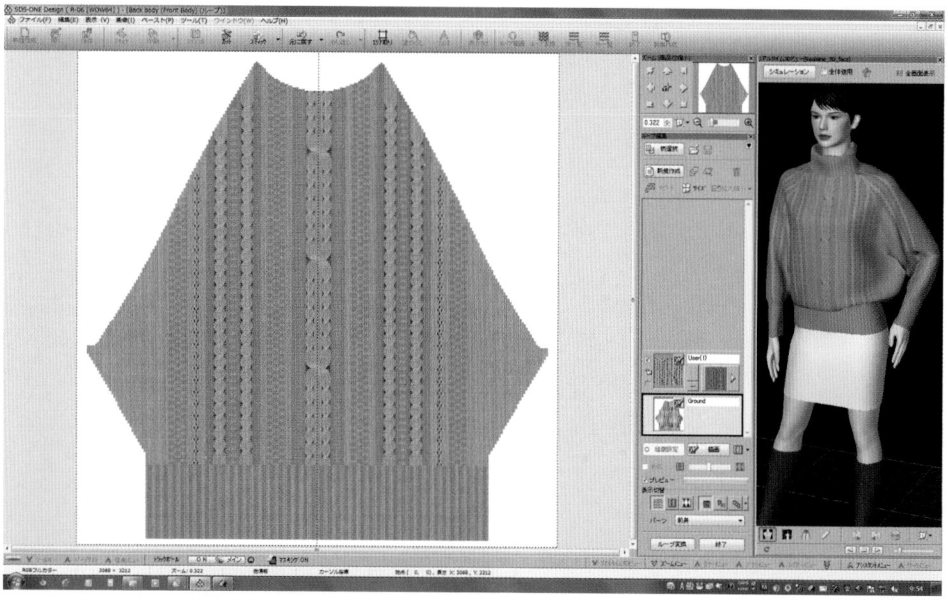

9

7. Flats worked up in alternative colourways using the Shima Seiki Apex system for textile design.

8. Knitwear digitally visualized flat and three-dimensionally prior to knitting.

9. The factory floor at Shima Seiki.

Sibling

Launched in 2008, Sibling is Joe Bates, Sid Bryan and Cozette McCreery. The East London knitwear trio release two collections each season and have been responsible for putting knitted pieces on the catwalk for numerous designers, including Alexander McQueen, Giles Deacon and Gareth Pugh. A piece of their crochet work, *Skull*, is in the collection of the Metropolitan Museum of Art in New York.

The revolutionary knitwear label started life as a menswear brand with the intention of 'kicking fashion up the arse', and has now spawned an accompanying womenswear label, Sister. Known for brightly coloured embellished knits, Sibling's designs combine Englishness and humour, alongside social context. They have embraced mixed disciplines, often collaborating with film-makers, photographers and artists to realize their ideas. Sibling show in Paris and London twice a year as part of Fashion Week.

What are your roles within the company?

To put it simply, Joe instigates the creative vision, Sid makes it real and Coz oversees how it is seen by the outside world.

Can you explain how you decide on each season's concept?

It is a process of elimination. When you are a working creative, many ideas constantly fly through your brain as possible usable concepts for a collection. It could be a photograph, a found garment or an abstract idea. Then you have to just grab one and start moving with it. If you find it doesn't give you enough creative fuel then you either add to it or ditch it and start with another.

How would you describe the design philosophy behind Sibling and Sister?

It is very important for us to retain our spirit of innovation and humour. The inspiration for starting the label in the first place was the lack of any true innovation in men's knitwear. We hope it is the wit of our collections that is most visible, but it is the intelligence of the product that makes it great design. We believe great design gets better the closer you look at it.

What keeps you designing knit?

The benefit of knit is that your starting point is a thread/yarn. Every piece is created from that most primitive point. It offers the most incredible freedom for a designer.

Can you describe your creative process, and how this is realized as products?

The creative process is 90 per cent editing. First, it is vital to have your concept, for this is the hook for everything that will happen creatively. So when you are steaming through ideas, they are always checked back: 'Does this sit with the concept?' If the answer is no, then it is put aside.

To truly develop any idea thoroughly, you need to push it, test it, edit. So thorough investigation through drawing is needed; it is here that quick, free, extreme experimentation can take place. Then edit again. Then into greater detail, greater precision, and another edit. Concurrent to this stage, swatching will start. Again, with the intention of broader experimentation, edit, then on to refining yarns, instilling further innovation within stitch.

When the collection is designed on paper and swatch, we have a line-up and make sure that the cohesion has not been lost. It is here that we edit out anything that is looking weak or superfluous. This is also the point to look to add in, when gaps in the range (line) are spotted.

At what stage of the design process do you consider materials and technologies?

These elements are often part of the initial concept, so from the very start. Other times it is when trying to solve a problem with traditional techniques that we will then be inspired to utilize a new technology to come up with an alternative solution.

Sibling has been involved in a number of collaborations. How do you decide who to work with?

We enjoy our collaborations. The selection is really quite simple: Does the company have a philosophy that we like/approve of? Will it be fun? Will it stretch the innovation skills of Sibling? If the answer is yes to these, then it's a winner.

How do you see Sibling and Sister developing?

We are fully aware that to grow we need to develop other product areas. However, we are enjoying where we are for the moment so we are in no rush. We are intending to be around for a long time and will take each business step only when we feel it is right.

83.

1

2

1. This sweater for Sister by Sibling features flowers embroidered in chunky yarn.

2. A two-piece skirt and cardigan ensemble is fully sequined and printed, accessorized with oversized knits.

3. Open stitchwork for a lightweight summer look.

4. Swarovski crystal is used to great effect in this lattice shift dress.

3

4

5

6

5. An exaggerated silhouette is created with embroidery.

6. This modern leopard print is an example of Sibling's playful use of scale.

7. A variety of knits on display at a Sibling spring/summer catwalk show.

7

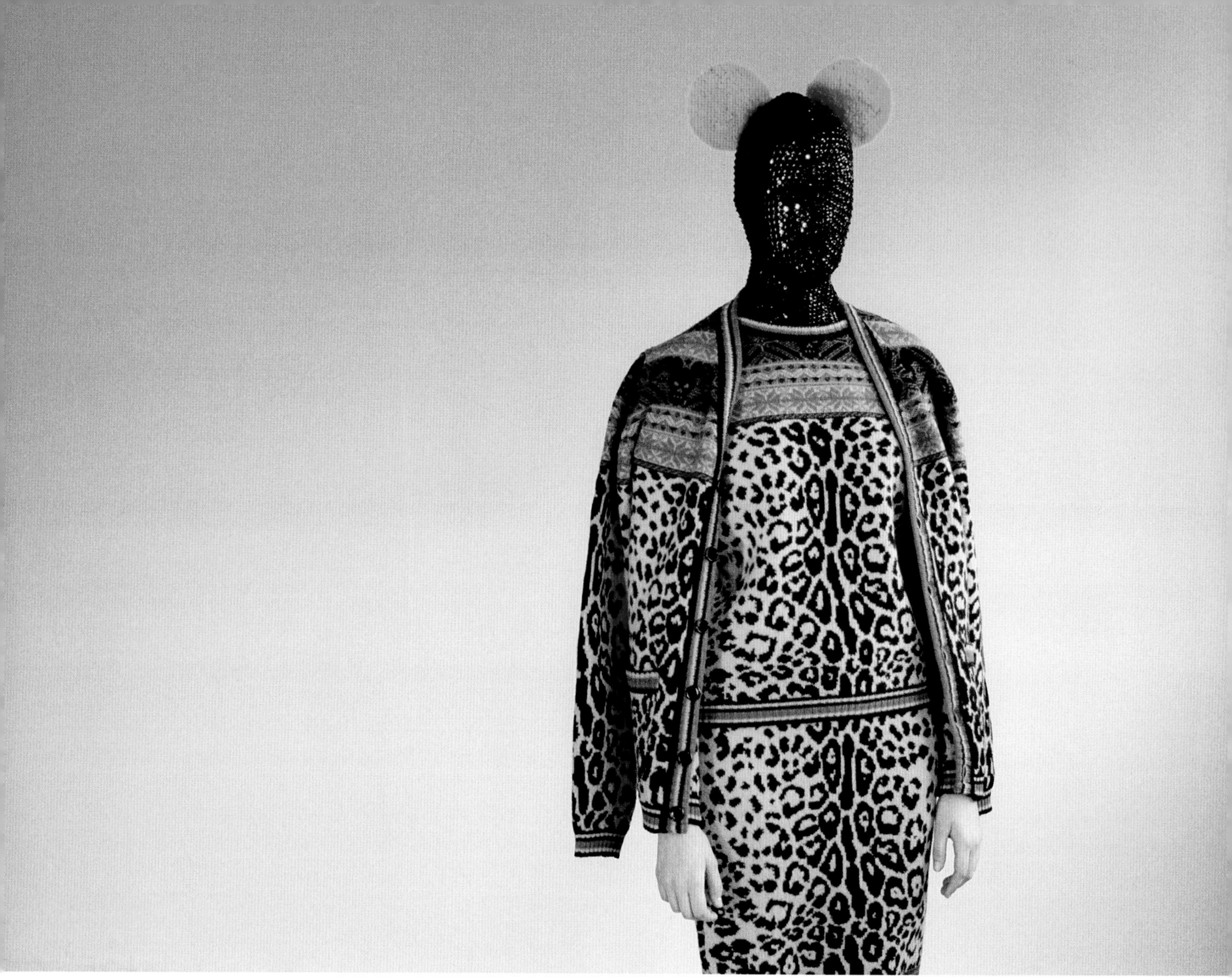

8

8. Sibling's Fair Isle leopard knit takes the twinset to the extreme.

9. Patterned knits in the Sibling show room.

Fashion: Sibling

9

Carlo Volpi

Carlo Volpi grew up in a small town near Florence, Italy, and moved to London at the age of nineteen. His introduction to dressmaking came through hanging out with club kids in the 1990s, spending the whole week making outfits to wear at the weekend.

Carlo studied for a BA in textiles at Goldsmiths College in London, continuing on to the Royal College of Art, graduating in textiles with a specialism in knit. Whilst at the RCA he received awards from both the Worshipful Company of Haberdashers and the Worshipful Company of Framework Knitters). His work was selected by Rowan Yarns to be exhibited at the department store Liberty during Wool Week 2012, and by Texprint to show in Paris at Première Vision. His current projects include research garments to be shown at the Italian yarn fair Pitti Filati. With his stitch-heavy, brightly coloured menswear pieces, he is definitely a designer to watch.

In addition to his fashion work, Carlo teaches hand-knit techniques to a broad range of students at London's Morley College, a community college with connections to such celebrated alumni as David Hockney. The course brings together knitters regardless of skill level, social standing, race or religion.

How long have you been knitting, and what inspired you to start?

I could kind of knit as a child. I grew up in near Prato, in Italy, and most families had at least one member who worked in the spinning or knitwear industry. Both my grandmothers worked in a small factory in my village, making hats (one of them still does, and she's over ninety now!). Manual crafts, however, were considered dirty work for uneducated people, so the younger generations were always pushed to do something 'better', like go to university, and many skills were lost.

It wasn't until I went to Goldsmiths that I started knitting again: we had a compulsory machine-knitting workshop, and the knitting machine brought all those childhood memories back. I haven't stopped since then!

Who comes to your group?

It varies every term. Morley's a great place. The people who come to the group are from very different backgrounds: some are retirees who want to learn new skills; others have stressful or difficult jobs, and want to do something relaxing. Others are young mums who want to learn how to make clothes for their kids, or office workers who have taken up knitting because it's fashionable at the moment.

Does anything else apart from knitting happen in your group?

I think for many students knitting is simply the common denominator to their very different lives, and it's very interesting to see how this craft is bringing people together. Knitting seems to loosen people up as well, so the conversation and the banter are always great.

How much do you think that environment affects design?

I think a designer's cultural background, the place where they grew up, where they live and work have a profound effect on what they make. The environment definitely has a strong impact on design.

Which techniques do you find to be the most popular?

I find that most beginners want to learn how to make cables, while more experienced learners want to learn how to adapt patterns.

Who has inspired you the most?

The one artist who has always inspired me is Leigh Bowery, who didn't actually knit. I find anybody with a debilitating obsession with knitting inspiring.

What's next for you?

I absolutely love collaborating with the Research Area at Pitti Filati: it is incredibly creative and it allows me to involve other designers and students in the realization of the pieces for the show. For the S/S 15 edition we worked with the knit students of Buckinghamshire New University, and for the next one I am contacting other designers and makers from different backgrounds. I find it is very beneficial for my students to be involved in this field, and it brings a fresh approach to my teaching.

I also work on the knitwear forecast for *Textile View* magazine, which gives me a chance to research new upcoming designers and craft people and promote their work in the magazine. I regularly write a blog on knittingindustry.com through which I promote the work of various people, from designers showing at fashion week to local makers and spinners.

I'm also collaborating with Dyloan Studio in Milan on a project that is aimed at bringing designers, spinners and knitwear factories together to push their new technologies (ultrasound and thermal welding, amongst others) and create something new that could potentially be used in industry.

91.

1

2

1. Volpi's 'Lipstick Stab Wounds' collection challenges stereotypical notions of masculinity with its reinterpretation of clothing from the traditionally male domain of sport. A mix of techniques, gauges and yarns adds interest to these knitwear pieces.

2. This dramatic statement piece from the same collection combines a stong cropped garment shape with unexpected details, such as the insert between the body and sleeve head.

4

3. Volpi is not afraid of using colour – something he also encourages his community of knitters to embrace. In this menswear piece from the 'Lipstick Stab Wounds' collection, bold, large-scale colourful motifs are interpreted through hand-knitting techniques.

4. A sweater from the same collection achieves contrast via technique, scale and gauge.

5

6

5, 6. Volpi's work on show at Pitti Filati, the yarn expo show held twice a year in Florence, Italy.

7

7. Volpi and his group of knitters hard at it during one of his classes. Knitters from all backgrounds, religions and social groups attend, the conversations cover all sorts of topics, and fun is had by all.

Christian Wijnants

Based in Antwerp, this Belgian designer is establishing a reputation for beautifully constructed garments that combine an interesting mix of stitch detail and dyeing techniques. Christian was the 2013 winner of the prestigious International Woolmark Prize (having previously won the European prize), which places him in the good company of such previous winners as Karl Lagerfeld and Yves Saint Laurent (see Woolmark, page 106). Stocked worldwide in renowned fashion stores – Barneys New York, Harvey Nichols in London, and Joyce in Hong Kong – the label is going from strength to strength.

How would you describe your work? Who buys your label?

Two words that best describe my aesthetic are 'soft' and 'poetic'. I like to develop fabrics that are not too stiff, using natural fibres. My clothes appeal to a wide range of women, although this can be a challenge as I have to consider a diverse range of ages and situations.

My brand has global appeal, and I have clients in America, Asia and Europe. What all my customers have in common is an appreciation of natural sophistication and a subtle femininity.

What keeps you designing knit?

There are many reasons. You can do so much with knitwear – you can experiment with the stitches. I love to take a thread and create something 3D which wraps around the body. As a designer you can define exactly what you want, and there are so many variations possible.

What is your role within the company?

It is half business and half creative – I find it an interesting mix. We now employ eight people, plus a group of freelancers. I work with stores, address the financial implications of running a business and also work as a creative, and it is a busy life.

Can you describe your creative thinking process, and how it is realized as products?

It starts with the research into textiles, the yarns and the knitted fabrics. I will often develop a knitted swatch and then work with this on the mannequin to inform silhouette. From this I then design the range (line). We work with both chunky and finer gauge.

Your pieces have a strong identity, with an emphasis on stitch detail and colour interest. At what stage of the design process do you consider materials and technologies?

Materials and the stitch are the starting points for my designs – deciding on the gauge of the knitting, and therefore whether it will be knitted on a machine or by hand, happens at the beginning of the process. Our shapes are informed by these developments. We have a few machines in-house and can sample and develop prototypes. We also experiment with dyeing and crochet. Our production is then outsourced, with industrial knits coming from Italy and hand knits coming from Croatia.

Our customers are very aware of quality – the feel of the yarns and a sense of luxury are fundamental to our core values as a brand.

Hand knit or machine knit?

Both – whatever is appropriate for the styling.

What effect has winning the International Woolmark Prize had on your business?

It has had a big impact – it has increased our brand visibility and acted as a great advertisement. It has been amazing to be associated with that fantastic label of quality. We had extensive coverage in the press attached to the win and this introduced me to new clients. And of course the prize money was amazing, and allowed me to invest in the company. Alongside all this, on a personal level it was very motivating to be recognized and to win such a prestigious prize.

Who has inspired you the most?

Having grown up in Belgium I was aware of the fashion greats, Martin Margiela and Dries Van Noten, from a very early age – they inspired me to follow in their footsteps. I studied fashion at the Royal Academy in Antwerp as they did; it made fashion seem like a real prospect and made me very proud.

How do you see the Christian Wijnants label developing?

We now show in Paris, and we plan to continue this. We aim to develop and increase our points of sale, to grow the brand, and eventually to develop the range (line) into accessories and menswear.

1

2

1. Stitch transfer results in an intricate lace in this delicate design.

2. Interest is created in this striped dress through the use of textured and marled yarns.

3

3, 4. These dresses, knitted seamlessly in merino wool and exploring techniques of dip and space dyeing, are part of a capsule collection that won Wijnants the 2013 International Woolmark Prize.

4

6

7

5. A classic heavy-guage knit, with clever use of stitch direction to add interest.

6, 7. Chunky yarn is used to advantage in these extreme furry knits.

Woolmark

The Woolmark symbol was created in 1964 and has been recognized globally ever since as a guarantee of quality, while the Woolmark Company continues to promote Australian merino wool as one of the world's most versatile and precious natural fibres. The company is now concentrating on new challenges, such as the need to educate a younger generation of consumers, the growth of emerging countries, and a focus on digital marketing and communications.

Approaching its fiftieth anniversary in 2014, the International Woolmark Prize remains a prestigious award, promoting wool and designers. Recipients include such luminaries as Yves Saint Laurent and Karl Lagerfeld, as well as the more recent winners featured in this book: Christian Wijnants (2013) and Sibling (2013 European winners and 2014 finalists). Rob Langtry is Chief Strategy and Marketing Officer of Australian Wool Innovation, of which the Woolmark Company is a subsidiary.

As a global brand how do you identify with your clients? Do you think there is a common language of design?

The core values of the brand – quality, innovation and respect for the environment – are very much aligned to the needs and desires of contemporary consumers, who are looking for a new idea of luxury which is both more authentic and eco-conscious.

Wool is an ancient fibre, worn by mankind for 10,000 years, with a great potential for the future, thanks to its unique natural qualities. Merino wool offers protection from the heat and the cold, elasticity, breathability, resilience, comfort and softness against the skin – it meets the demands of a global, cosmopolitan and discerning consumer perfectly.

What upcoming trends or areas of interest can you identify in knit?

We see two main trends at the moment: the first is extreme and sculptural knitwear, where the focus is on volumes, with either a cocooning or a protective effect; the other is superfine, ultra-light and transparent knits, which exploit the breathability and elasticity of the fibre, increasing the usage of the finest wool yarns in Spring/Summer collections. Both these trends are present in the Wool Lab Autumn/Winter 2014–15.

The Wool Lab is a trend book and sourcing guide for fashion and textile industry professionals, produced twice a year in collaboration with the world's best weavers and spinners.

Your Wool School successfully unites professional bodies and educational institutions in the UK. Can you describe the success of the programme?

Wool School, conceived under the umbrella of the Campaign for Wool, is based on the idea that we have to feed and educate the upcoming generation of fashion professionals, in order to ensure that values like excellence, creativity and respect for the environment are consistent across the supply chain. It has been a great success because of its capacity to provide school and university students with a business experience – the garments they create are showcased by top global retail brands who are partners of the project, and some are made commercially available. Education is a key area in which we will continue to experiment and invest.

What have been your most successful or interesting collaborations?

The co-branded campaigns under 'Merino Wool. No Finer Feeling' have achieved maximum cut-through. The merino wool ambassadors we have worked with over the past three years include Giorgio Armani, Vivienne Westwood, Missoni, Ermenegildo Zegna, Loro Piana and Alexander Wang, each of whom has created PR opportunities through their individual product development and fibre endorsement, attracting the attention of both industry and consumers alike. The influence of the designers and the reach at a consumer level cannot be matched.

How do you select designers for the Woolmark Prize shortlist?

Designers are nominated by 19 global bodies, each selected by the Woolmark Company as the most credible experts in the fashion industry: they include the British Fashion Council, the Council of Fashion Designers of America (CFDA), Not Just a Label and *Vogue Italia*.

Another element in assuring the quality of the competition and the highest level of participants is the choice of judges. We have been fortunate to have featured the most influential names in fashion, such as Alber Elbaz, Donatella Versace, Diane von Furstenberg, Franca Sozzani, Carla Sozzani, Paula Reed and, more recently, Alexander Wang and Angela Missoni.

Amongst the most important winners we are proud to mention Yves Saint Laurent and Karl Lagerfeld, who won the competition in 1954, its inaugural year. At that time, the competition was run by the International Wool Secretariat, the former global association of wool producers.

What next for Woolmark?

The Woolmark Company is naturally evolving on the basis of the market's needs and trends. We will continue to invest in marketing activities in order to affirm wool's position as a premium fibre within the global fashion system.

1

2

3

1. The Woolmark symbol, created in 1964, is a globally recognized trademark.

2. This press piece created for Woolmark reflects the journey of wool from the sheep's back to fine knitwear.

3. A merino fleece in its raw state.

5

4, 5. Woolmark advocates the versatility and luxury of merino wool in menswear and womenswear, both classic and casual. The company often works in collaboration with designers, who act as merino wool ambassadors.

6

6. Woolmark's 'Cool Wool' campaign highlighted wool's ability to offer insulation from heat.

7. Woolmark promotes pure new wool as a premium natural fibre around the world. The Woolmark logo is seen here in Place de Clichy in Paris.

PURE LAINE VIERGE
PURE LAINE VIERGE
PURE LAINE VIERGE
PURE LAINE VIERGE
PATHE
WEPLER
GAUMONT

Art

The contributors included in this section use knit as a medium to explore a range of different techniques and themes, but what they have in common is the ability to inspire, and a desire to avoid being pigeonholed in any one category. Most have trained in another discipline, or are combining other interests with knit; all are adaptable, enthusiastic and driven by a passion to produce very special works.

As a craft traditionally performed by women, knitting is often adopted and subverted to redefine the feminine, frequently expressing strength and defiance. Historical context, female subjugation, technique, emotions and social commentary are all explored using knitted forms by these very different practitioners.

Because of the nature of the stitch and the use of a continuous thread, knitted fabrics are very strong and can be used to support large structures. Annette Streyl, who originally trained as a stonemason, explores architecture, working on a scale of 1:100 to create soft replicas of static monoliths that invite viewers to embrace architecture in a totally different way, equally as fascinating draped as when taught over frames.

Two London-based artists – Chia-Shan Lee and Na'ama Rietti – are showcased. Both are heavily influenced by their Taiwanese and Middle-Eastern heritages respectively and draw on this to fuel original art pieces.

Having learned to knit while at college, Danish artist Isabel Berglund now uses the medium to create objects and installations that defy categorization, while the work of Australian artist Ruth Marshall focuses very much on her chosen subject – endangered wildlife.

The knitted works featured in this section are not restricted to the traditional gallery environment either. Liz Collins and her Knitting Nation troupe perform site-specific pieces that explore issues relating to labour and the human body, while Magda Sayeg – the (very youthful!) grandmother of yarn bombing – speaks frankly about the movement she created, and how it has morphed into a very different phenomenon. Lauren O'Farrell (aka Deadly Knitshade) situates her works on the streets of London, making them accessible and available to all; her 'Stitch London' group, which she co-founded, now has over 10,000 members.

Knitting that appears in unexpected environments, knitting that masquerades, as something it is not, knitting that provokes questions – this is when knitting becomes art.

B-Arbeiten

The German guerrilla knitting group known as B-Arbeiten – an adaptation of the German word meaning 'to edit' or 'to alter' – are known for using yarn bombing to decorate public objects such as trees and ferries and, more recently, to create tipi structures.

Founding member Ute Lennartz-Lembeck is a textile artist with a background in art and education. She is inspired by human desires; her observations on philosophy, psychology, economics, meditation and social interaction inform her knitted structures, and the concepts behind her work are reaffirmed by collaborative working.

How long have you been knitting, and what inspired you to adopt knit as your medium?

I have always knitted and crocheted. The production process has meditative traits which contribute to a 'deceleration' in what is, in my view, a very oversaturated world. In addition, these techniques are anchored in our culture and have a true sustainability and a political significance.

Does your environment have an effect on your work?

The soft material, which is representative of warmth, the often cold public space – all this was becoming more and more interesting to me. Through my interests I then came to 'urban knitting'. It started with fixing small 'wool works' in various places. The meditative process of making and placing work in public spaces, both real and virtual, has since enabled me to develop links with like-minded people.

Your work seems very concept-driven. Can you expand on this?

The significance of concepts and values can, in my view, often be very inflationary (both globally as well as domestically); 'values' are preceded by intensive philosophical research. Values are the same everywhere, independent of skin colour, social status or place of residence.

You embrace collaboration with other knitters. How do you manage this, and what effect does it have on the final works?

I have been assisted partly by friends and partly by family, but also by strangers, whom I have met through social networks. This has resulted in pictures that have documented the fixing and installation, but also in many stories. The people who install the works are involved in the creations and experiences; they in turn have new encounters with passers-by and engage in conversations. The pictures of the work are then shared worldwide via Facebook, thus giving rise to further new encounters.

'Tipis' is a project that embraces several social organizations. How do you see this developing, and where would it be based?

The first tipi created a buzz, and the idea of collaboration arose. It started with a self-help group in Cologne, an institution that looks after young people. What was appealing was the creation of many individual squares – everyone can do that, everywhere. I support and accompany every project photographically, documenting manually, and I try to find sponsors by applying for public tenders or competitions.

I have since continued working with the tipi. I chose this form because I wanted to create a three-dimensional space that was transparent and created a link between inside and outside – visibly and via the senses – palpably linking the emotional with the tangible. The tipi is also about reusability and mobility.

My wish would be for a small village, where all the tipis would stand. I have at my disposal a large, wild piece of land. There, in the summer, you could have one week when all the tipis would be erected; there is space for camping, and each group would be able to hold workshops, to connect further, with special spaces and rooms.

What do you consider to be your most successful piece of work, and is this also your favourite?

I try to create fabrics, in particular; in general, I try to document, represent, question and live them. It is a movement, which is why I cannot have a favourite object. All the works have their own specific significance and meaning.

What next for you?

I would like to document the progress of the 'Tipis' project in written form. At the moment I work on this in parallel, but I want to simplify the form – it does not require 'big words' – and establish it as a work in its own right.

1

2

1. 'Tipis' is an ongoing collaborative project that is now housed in seven different locations, including Basel, Cologne and Remscheid. There is a German tour planned, and an installation village to follow. To form each tipi, panels are meticulously sewn together by hand.

2. Tipis work equally well as indoor installations. Here the Remscheid tipi is shown in situ at the 2013 h&h (handicrafts and hobbies) trade fair in Cologne.

3. Detail of a project with graffiti-knitting group Basel farbARTig verstriggt (which translates as 'Basel knitted colourARTfully').

Gelassenheit
DIE WAHRE LIEBE
KINDER

5

6

4. Known as the Traueweide (weeping willow), this tree has a new dress comprised of over 350 knitted sections, collected from a worldwide set of contributors.

5. The Basel–Münster ferry, yarn-bombed by Ute and graffiti knitting group Basel farbARTig verstriggt.

6. A yarn-bombed car. B-Arbeiten have given a similar treatment to other vehicles, including tanks and bicycles.

7

8

7, 8. A yarn-bombed urban space in Padua, Italy.

9. A 60-metre-long (197-foot-long) knitted installation at Eschbach Dam in Remscheid, Germany – the first dam built in Germany for drinking water. The project aimed to raise awareness of natural water resources.

123.

9

Isabel Berglund

Isabel Berglund is an artist who has adopted knit as her medium, and she describes her work as being 'between categories such as design, art and fashion'. Her sculptural pieces have an arresting presence, manifesting in unique and unexpected original forms, ranging from a knitted forest, which can absorb the viewer in a fantasy world created from wool, to a stark, clean white chair housed in a wardrobe, to strange abstract creations. A graduate of Central Saint Martins in London, Isabel has exhibited globally at numerous shows, and has had work included in influential publications.

You have commented that your work sits between recognized categories. How do you define yourself?

I am an artist, but my work is about asking questions of everyday objects in relation to people. Therefore, I think it is important not to choose categories. When I see pieces at exhibitions located in between categories, it always gives me a greater curiosity, and that's what I like to achieve with my own projects.

How long have you been knitting, and what inspired you to adopt knit as your medium?

I started hand-knitting whilst at Central Saint Martins. At the time I did not know how to hand-knit; I remember that it was a nice Yugoslavian woman who worked as a seamstress at the school who taught me how to knit by hand.

Does your environment have an effect on your work?

The environment inspires me – everyday life, people, words and objects. I work on projects that relate to the body and sex, on the border between function and abstract thinking, hard and soft, the recognizable and unexpected. I find it interesting to work with everyday objects put together with puns and concepts.

Part of my work is about creating a dialogue between the story I see in the concrete object and the story that I will make with the sculpture.

How do you start a project, and how do you progress it?

I always start with the idea of a concrete object seen in a new context and thereby make a word game and a new story of the sketches on the computer. Here I work with the balance of the knitted shape and mass, and with conceptual and narrative presence and absence.

Language is a dimension of my work. With a piece like *Can You Handle Me*, for example, I took the title literally and displayed a handle. The same work is also a good example of how I incorporate multiple contradictions: function and abstraction, hard and soft, presence and absence, such as the cavities one senses in the objects but cannot see. On the one hand, the work is tangible; on the other it is an image, a symbol, and thereby also acts on our perception of reality.

What other materials do you use – are you tempted to broaden the range?

I love to work with contrast. I also make sculptures in wood and soft knitted material – these two contradictory materials inspire each other in the three-dimensional shape of my sculptures.

Collaboration or autonomy – what works best for you?

I do both. I really like to work in different settings with a project; it inspires me.

What do you consider to be your most successful piece of work, and is this also your favourite?

My favourite piece is often the latest project I have made. But the project that has been most viewed and has travelled most around in the world is *City of Stitches and Wood*, my knitted room from 2005. There were so many people involved in the creation of this project, both hand-knitting and stitching the pieces together (as with *Knitted Green Pollution*, 2009).

Who or what inspires you the most?

People, words, objects, art, design, fashion and movies.

What happens to your pieces?

Some pieces are sold; others are either in exhibitions around the world or stored in my studio.

What next for you?

Great new and inspiring projects – I am currently working on sketches for an exhibition later this year, and I am participating in many exhibitions coming up in various countries around the world, including Korea, Japan, Germany and France.

125.

1

Art: Isabel Berglund

Art: Isabel Berglund

3

4

1. Berglund at work on a knitted piece.

2. *Can You Handle Me*, 2011.

3. *Falling*, 2012.

4. Moulds used to shape *Falling*.

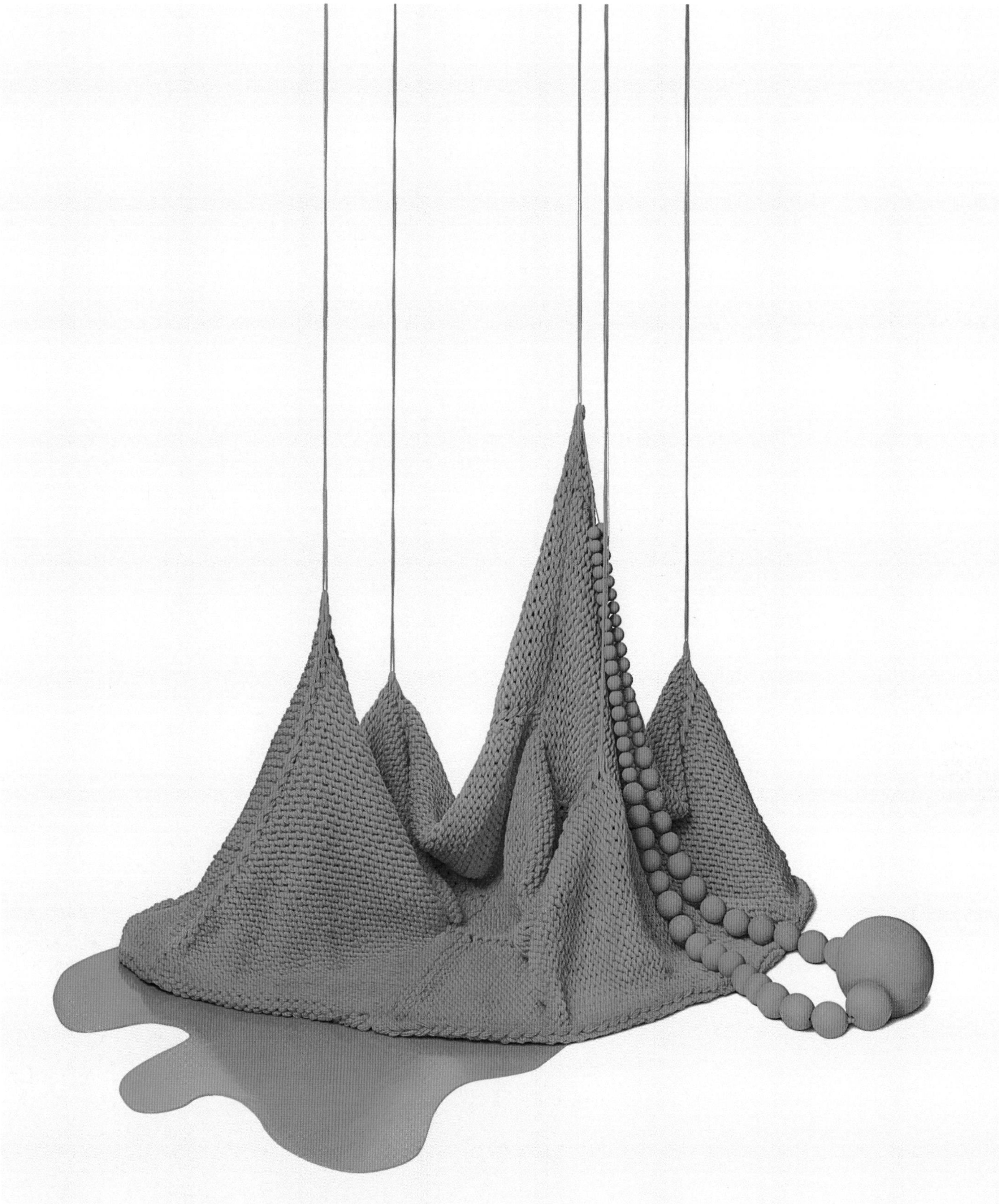

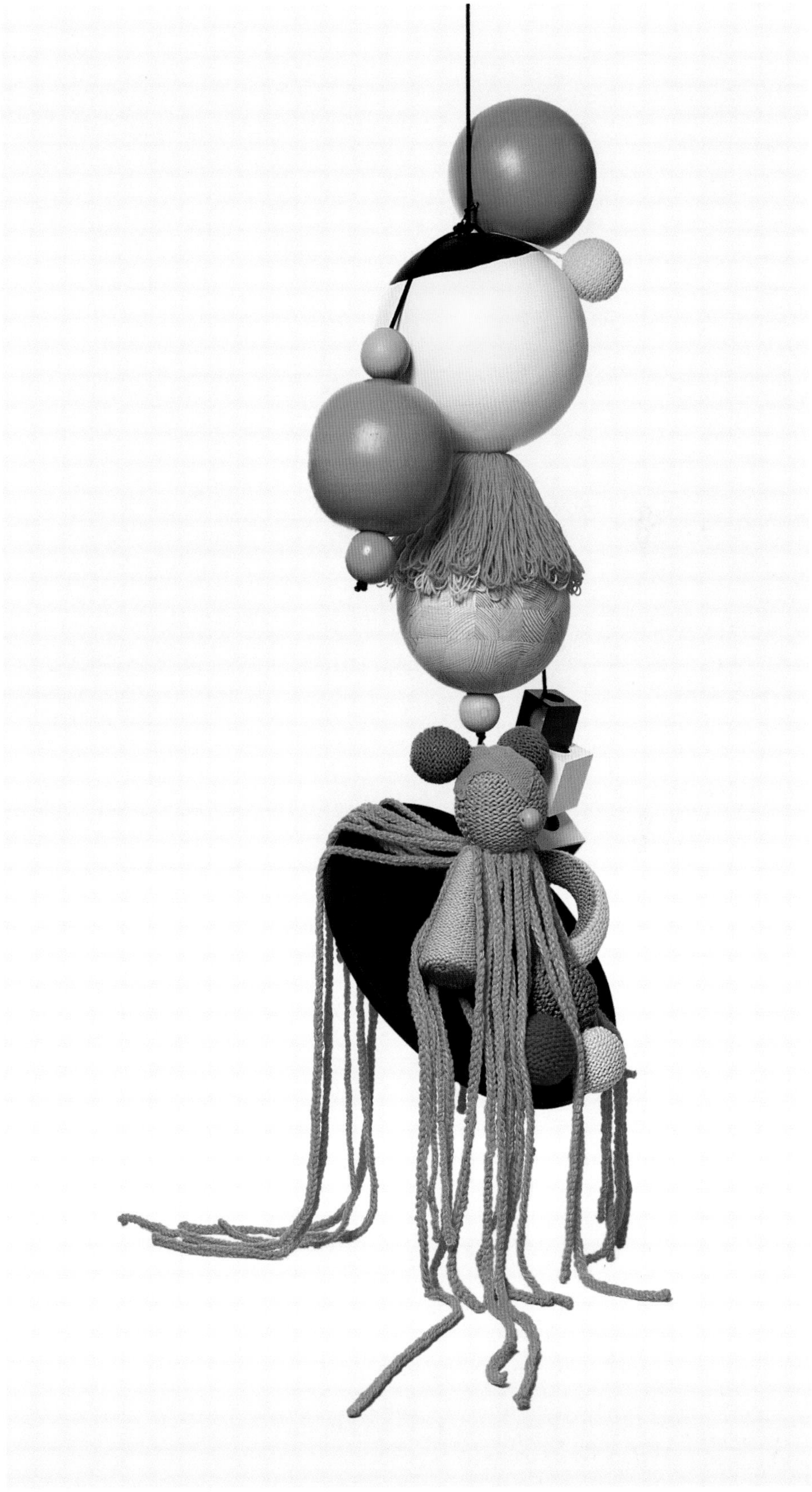

6

5. *Floating Pearls*, 2011.

6. *Electric Knit Trip*, 2009.

7

7. *City of Stitches and Wood*, 2005.

8. *Knitted Green Pollution*, 2009.

Art: Isabel Berglund

Liz Collins

Liz Collins is a textile artist based in New York, who uses knit as her tool to communicate ideas relating to sexuality and the industrialization of craft. Liz graduated from the Rhode Island School of Design (RISD) in Providence in the 1990s, and her output has been prolific since then. Her diverse range of work, which has been exhibited at numerous shows in the USA, challenges and provokes debate. Liz is best known for Knitting Nation, a performance and site-specific installation project that she set up, which stages various 'knit interventions', often documented on film.

Liz also has a background in the fashion industry, designing a range (line) under her own name, and she teaches at both the Pratt Institute in New York and at RISD, where she holds the position of associate professor.

Your work is very diverse and seems to embrace craft/art as well as installation and social reflection. How do you define yourself and your work?

You just did a good job defining it, except you left off fashion. I self-identify as an artist and designer specializing in knits – or a knitwear designer and multimedia artist who often uses machine-knitting as a tool of aesthetic and cultural enquiry. I am starting to do more works outside of knitting these days, so I am having to redefine myself with less of a specialization.

It's always interesting to have a hybrid practice. I have to define my work more as an artist/art, rather than a fashion designer/fashion, before I can be taken seriously. There are people in the art world who are great supporters of my work and understand how the fashion feeds the art, and vice versa.

How long have you been knitting, and what inspired you to adopt knit as your medium?

I have been machine-knitting since 1997 and hand-knitting since 1992. Before knitting I was weaving. I learned to hand-knit and quickly understood the power of it. I could make highly wearable fabric and form in one concurrent process with no set-up time. I haven't woven since. Knitting offered all I needed.

How do you start a project, and how do you progress it?

It depends on the project. My narratives are often intuitive and ongoing and find their ways into my work whether I am trying to put them there or not. They underlie everything.

Can you explain the philosophy behind knitting interventions and your work with Knitting Nation?

Knitting Nation functions as a platform for me to explore many things. It has some fixed elements – the knitting machines; the live, uniformed/costumed labour; the site-specific response to a space/site with the building of something. I am looking at physical endurance in relation to human labour, the rigour and demands of labour, the dance of labour and repetitive motion.

The knitting 'interventions' are based on the idea that I can intervene in the state of an object, usually wearable, and thus change it into something different.

What do you consider to be your most successful piece of work, and is this also your favourite?

Knitting Nation Phase 7: Darkness Descends at the Institute of Contemporary Art in Boston in 2011. It was perfect and led me into a trance state, in part because it was beautiful and powerful. The regimented, dark, militaristic, sexy, glam, tough, formal, high-drama qualities of it were stunning to me. And to be in it so fully with my body and to see four other fierce women in the same state in the five-pointed star.

Who or what has inspired you the most?

I am inspired and driven by materials and process. I am motivated not only by the act and history of knitting itself, but I also receive inspiration from nature, the internal and external architecture of the human body, and our emotional and physical experiences as humans.

Across techniques and media, frequent themes of my work include decay, wounds, layers, bondage, and the many anatomical forms and systems found in plants and animals, including humans.

You also teach. Does this influence your practice?

Through teaching I have learned more advanced knit structures and technology. I spent one month in Germany learning to program and run Stoll machines, so that we could build the knitting curriculum at RISD.

I don't think Knitting Nation would have emerged without teaching, as it was a knitting lab full of students on domestic flatbed machines that gave me the impetus to form a group of knitters. It was an automatic workforce of people who, like me, love art and knitting and were game to do new things. The project is endlessly fed by students, alumni and colleagues. So teaching has been essential to the work.

What next for you?

Knitting Nation Phase 12: H2O took place at Occidental College in LA in November 2013, and more performance/events/installations/shows in New York City and beyond will inevitably follow in the future. I am also in the beginning stages of starting a knit art/design collective in Brooklyn. It's going to be full of talent and great projects.

1

2

3

1. *Knitting Nation Phase 4: Pride*, 2007, multimedia, durational performance/installation in Providence, Rhode Island, USA.

2. *Knitting Nation Phase 8: Under Construction*, 2011, multimedia, durational performance/installation at the Institute of Contemporary Art, Boston.

3. *Knitting Nation Phase 7: Darkness Descends*, 2011, multimedia, durational performance/installation at the Institute of Contemporary Art, Boston.

4

4. *Knitting Nation Phase 10: Domestic Swarming*, 2012, multimedia, durational performance/ installation and collaborative response to and engagement with Fritz Haeg's *Domestic Integrities* rug installation at the Museum of Modern Art, New York.

6

5. *Reflective Mesh Sweater*, 2009, hand-knitted cashmere, angora, silk, reflective silt film; and *Reflective Ribcage Dress*, 1999, hand-loomed silk and reflective slit film.

6. *Illuminated Veins*, 2009, hand-loomed and grafted silk and reflective slit film with silk organza.

7

7. *Sock Monkey Suit*, 2009, hand-loomed wool/cashmere/silk (chair by Alphonse Mattia).

8. *Hole and Bubble Sweaters*, 2013, hand-loomed baby alpaca and silk.

Art: Liz Collins

Chia-Shan Lee

Chia-Shan was born in Taiwan, and is currently based in London. Having trained in textile design in both Taiwan and in the UK, she now identifies herself as an artist. Since 2010 she has used spun newspaper – or 'newspaper yarn' – to create installations and wearable art. Due to the nature of the material, these works capture stories of our time, presented through the eyes of the artist, and focus on the issues of waste and sustainability.

Chia-Shan's series of installations titled *The Never Ending Story* won the One Hundred Days contest in 2012. This is an annual international competition for emerging artists, held in New York and sponsored by the experiential arts organization Contaminate. Chia-Shan's first solo exhibition was also held in New York in 2012.

How long have you been knitting, and what inspired you to adopt knit as your medium?

My mum taught me how to knit when I was nine years old. It was a plain navy scarf that I still cherish. I fell in love with knitting, the texture of knitting. It is special and creative: from a single thread you can create any texture, shape and structure. I enjoy the process of knitting, too; for me, it is symbolic of slow craft, time for reflection – knitting in a message.

Knitting for me is just like a composition. People use letters to make words, and use words to create sentences, and then go on to create articles. I knit a beautiful installation by knitting single loops to make a piece of work.

How do you start a project, and how do you progress it?

I start with concepts or ideas drawn from my daily life and my background. I am an Asian girl living in London, one of the busiest and most international cities in the world. Unfamiliar countries, different cultures, foreign languages and words – all these things inspire me. I also always tell myself to dream my dreams and keep a curious mind.

Can you explain how you use newspaper to produce your pieces?

I slice newspapers into strips and then spin these strips into newspaper yarns. I then use hand-knit needles or crochet hooks to shape these handmade yarns into all sorts of 3D installations without using frames. The installations are quite hard and strong, and the texture of the newspaper yarn is unique.

I am interested in employing newspaper yarns as a narrative material because the viewer can then appreciate the meaning of the words that appear in the paper. The yarns record news and events, and reflect current social situations. A viewer may not be able to read a full article; however, I want people to sense the abstract meaning of the words.

What other materials do you use? Are you tempted to broaden the range?

At this moment, the main material is newspaper, assisted by some vibrant wool yarns to add colour.

Hand knit or machine knit?

I mostly hand-knit and crochet – both processes are slower, but they have fewer limits and can create more creative textures, structures and shapes.

What do you consider to be your most successful piece of work, and is this also your favourite?

The Never Ending Story is my favourite series of works, and I do consider it my most successful. The project was inspired by the paper waste associated with newspaper production, which in turn inspired me to make a link between my knitting technique and recycling issues.

I decided to use my aesthetic skills and knowledge to create some contemporary pieces, which would allow people to understand how much paper we waste and how serious this issue is. Moreover, the aim was to try and engage with people who are not interested in environmental issues.

Who or what has inspired you the most?

Travelling. Different places and different views inspire me a lot. I always try to imagine what has happened in this ancient stone house, or try to figure out the meaning of foreign letters.

How do you define yourself?

I prefer to say I am an artist. I put the focus on my artworks, although I have a fashion and textile-design background. I worked in a fashion apparel company as an assistant knitwear designer for two years, and now I am a technical knit consultant for Apu Jan (an English-based Taiwanese designer brand). I like to use my artworks to communicate both ideas and information.

What next for you?

I am now an MFA student at the Wimbledon College of Art. I am also planning to run a project called 'Open This Page', and want to invite other global travellers to join me by sending me newspapers from all around the world. These newspapers, consisting of memories of journeys and stories, will create a new story – a fantastic and adventurous journey.

Encourage us to open this page.

1

2

1. Bird detail from Chia-Shan's installation series *The Never Ending Story*, 2011.

2, 3. Other pieces from *The Never Ending Story*. The collection is knitted from newspaper fashioned into yarn.

Art: Chia-Shan Lee

4

5

6

4, 5, 6. Chia-Shan's newspaper yarn has no stretch, so creating these intricate lace stitches takes time and skill.

7

8

9

7. Dyeing a knitted newspaper swatch.

8. In this close-up shot, the newspaper origins of Chia-Shan's yarn is visible.

9. Newspaper yarn on knitting needles. Chia-Shan hand-knits and crochets her handmade newspaper yarn into intricate and delicate constructions.

Ruth Marshall

Ruth Marshall was born and raised in Australia, but has also travelled extensively. After graduating from art school she was awarded the prestigious Anne and Gordon Samstag International Visual Arts scholarship; this was used to fund a degree at the Pratt Institute in New York.

Ruth worked for 14 years at the Bronx Zoo as an exhibit sculptor, which had a profound and lasting influence on her love of nature and wildlife. She now teaches and dedicates her time to her work, creating pieces supported by artist residencies, museum research, lectures and workshops. She recently had her first solo museum show, and published her first book.

How long have you been knitting, and what inspired you to adopt knit as your medium?

I've knitted ever since I was a child. My mother and my aunt taught me to knit in tandem and I knitted profusely as a child until I was a teenager and lost interest. It took two art degrees to circle back to my roots in craft and knitting in order to see it as a viable medium to create art with. Rediscovering knitting as an adult reminded me of all those childhood pleasures.

Does your environment have an effect on your work?

The environment of the Bronx Zoo was pivotal in the development of my art – the animals there and being constantly surrounded and educated about species survival inspired me to refocus my subject matter, medium and concepts.

How do you start a project, and how do you progress it?

It starts with the animals – ones that have a dynamic pattern, whether they are endangered or threatened as a species, and whether I can study a specimen of the animal in a museum or have access to one in a zoo that I can photograph. It can depend on where I am and what is available.

Which stitches and yarns do you favour?

Because I do coloured knitting – intarsia, which is sometimes combined with Fair Isle – I use very plain knitting or stocking stitch, so no fancy stitches. The colours are where the complexity lies. I do also try to use 100 per cent wool or natural yarns.

Your work seems to bridge the divide between craft/art and education. Have you had any interesting experiences relating to this?

Yes, I love talking to children about my work. They get it, and they get so excited learning about interesting facts to do with coral snakes or tigers, although we usually end up talking about ligers [a cross between a male lion and a tigress] and white tigers. What I have learned is that people really do care about these animals; they don't want species like tigers to disappear, but they feel powerless, so I try to give out information about the animals and organizations so at least they have some tools and knowledge if they choose to take action.

Artist or archivist?

Artist first, which I believe would then lead directly into archival activities.

What do you consider to be your most successful piece of work, and is this also your favourite?

Well it's always the last piece completed, right? But my other favourite is *#6 Ocelot*. This pelt is based on a little female ocelot that lived in a New York City zoo back in the late 1890s. That pelt really spoke to me. It was amazing to think that the soft fur I studied was once inhabited by a living animal over 100 years ago.

You also teach. Does this influence your practice?

Teaching has helped to teach me that I have skills to share with art students. There are so many abstract and conceptual elements to being an artist that it can seem that you have nothing really substantial to offer. Teaching provides a wonderful opportunity to share the mindset of an artist with these young people, and I always feel the best thing I have to offer as a teacher is verbalizing my thoughts and teaching them how to think like an artist. So I think it is more of a case of how my practice affects my teaching.

One of my strengths as an artist is that I've learnt to always trust my own gut reaction to my work, and I've found that I can bring that intuition, forthrightness and directness to my analysis and criticism of student work. I'm usually right and they usually agree.

What next for you?

I am about to begin a series of Australian animals – very small Leadbeater's possums and striped possums, bandicoots, numbats, quolls and the extinct Tasmanian tiger – so I think it will be an interesting look into the unusual flora that exists and is currently threatened in Australia. Apart from that I just want to keep working and developing as an artist. Once you've begun sniffing along that trail you never know where it will lead.

149.

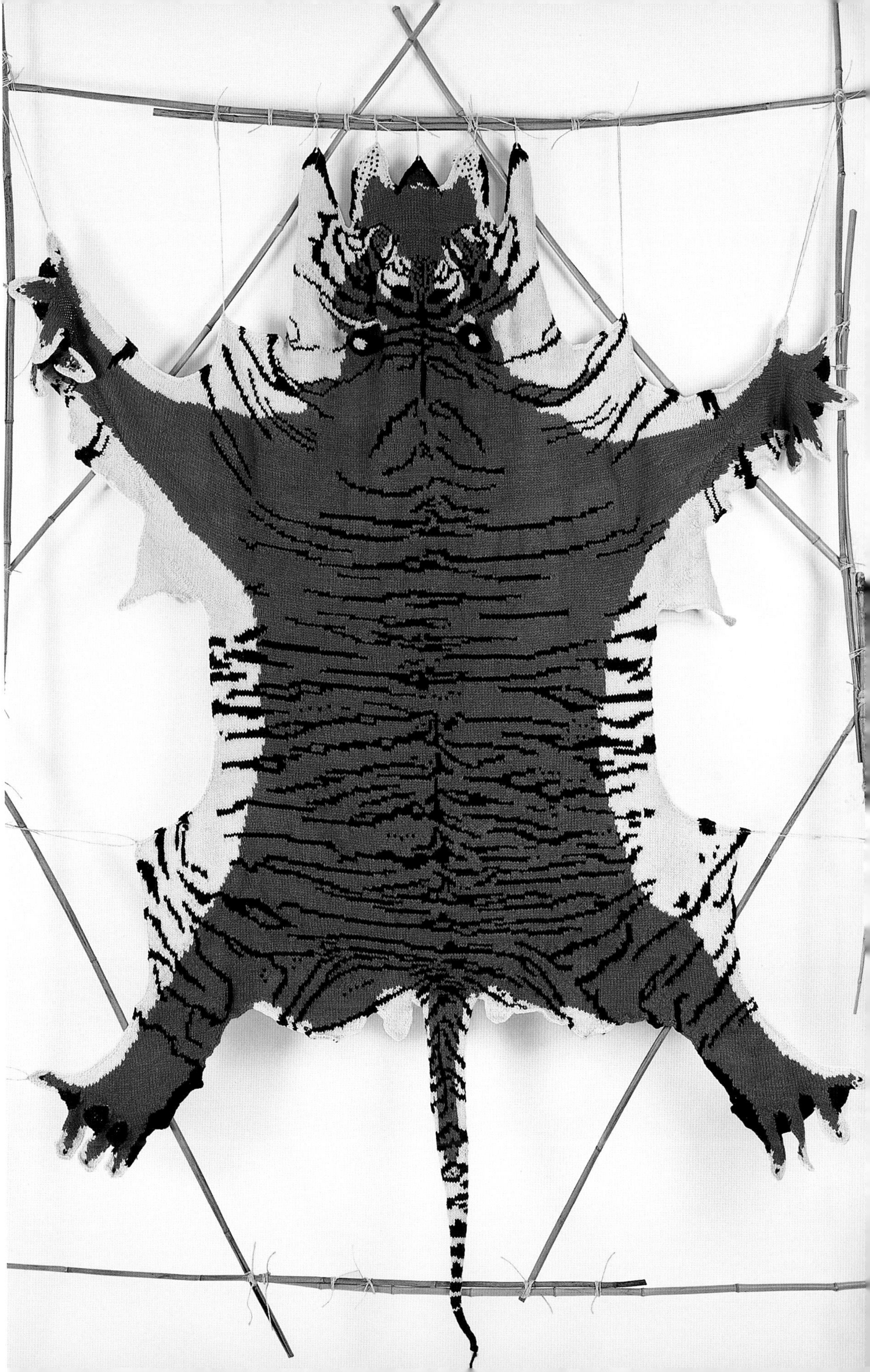

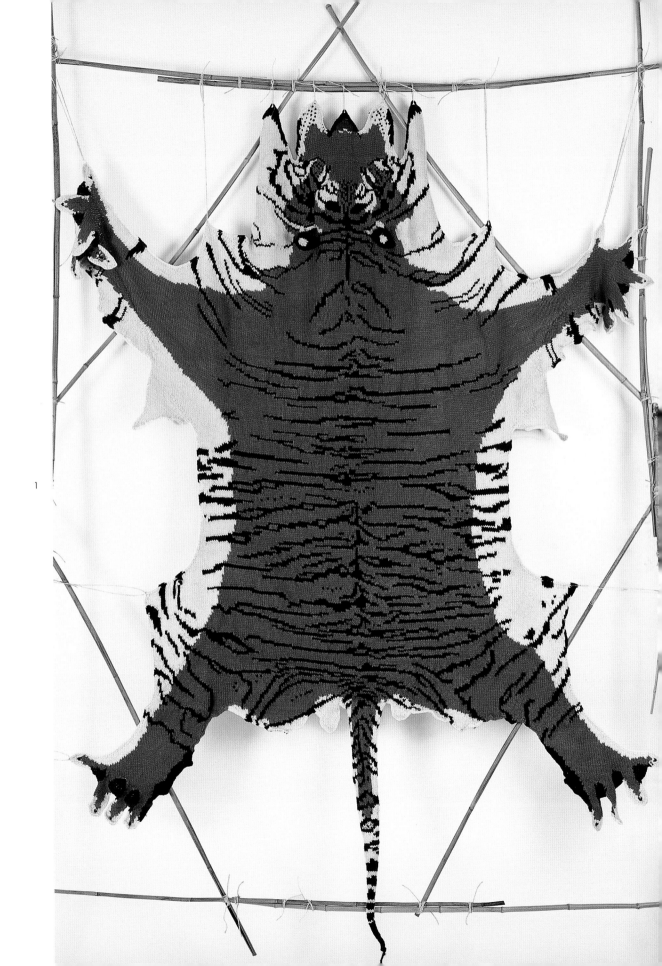

2

1. *Female Berlin Tiger*, 2012.

2. Wall of tigers at the 'Vanished into Stitches' exhibition at the University of Maine, Bangor, Museum of Art, 2012. The curating idea behind the show was to have the work lashed onto the bamboo frames overlapping and crowded into the gallery space for an overwhelming experience.

3, 4. Design and planning drawings for one of Marshall's tigers.

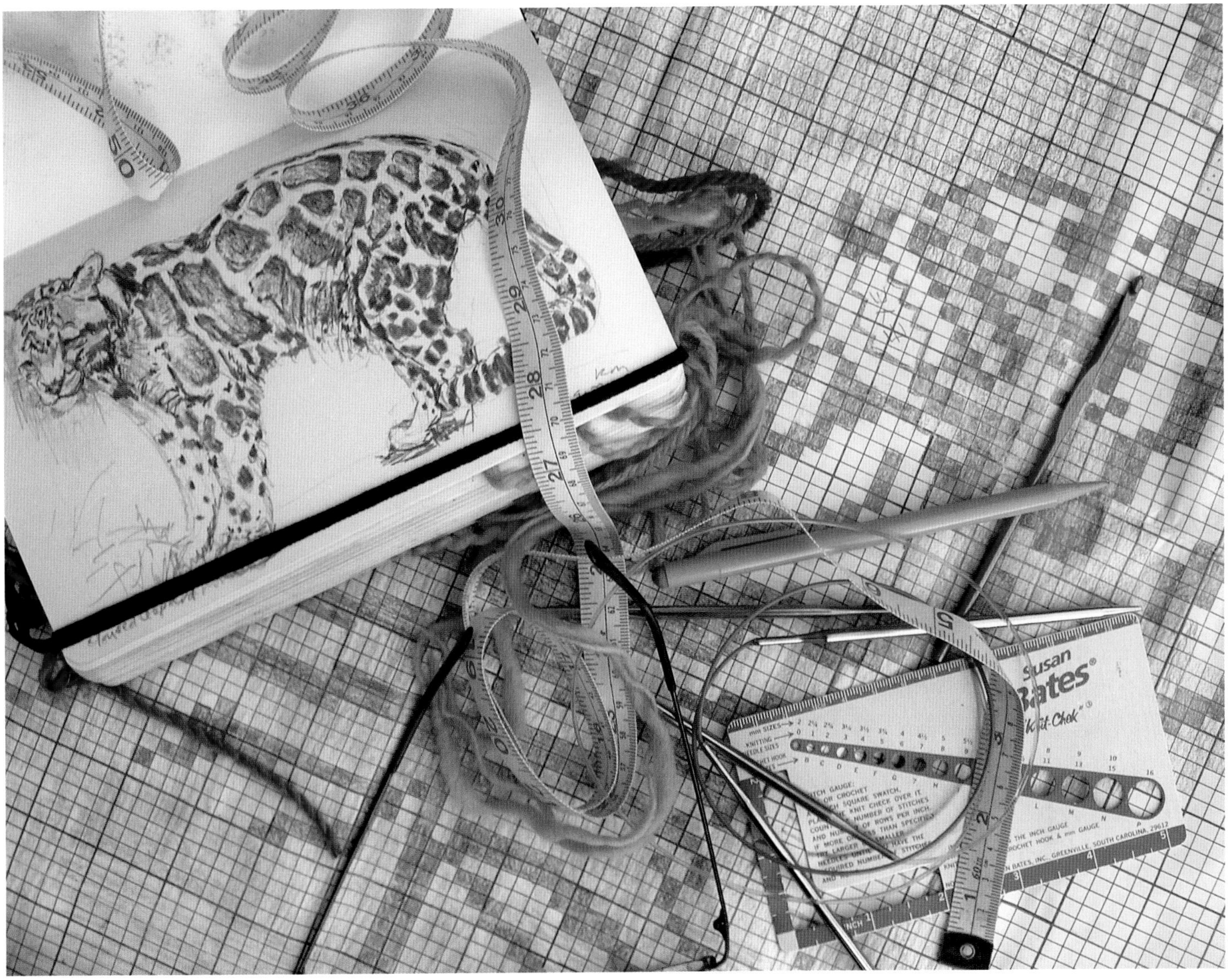

3

4

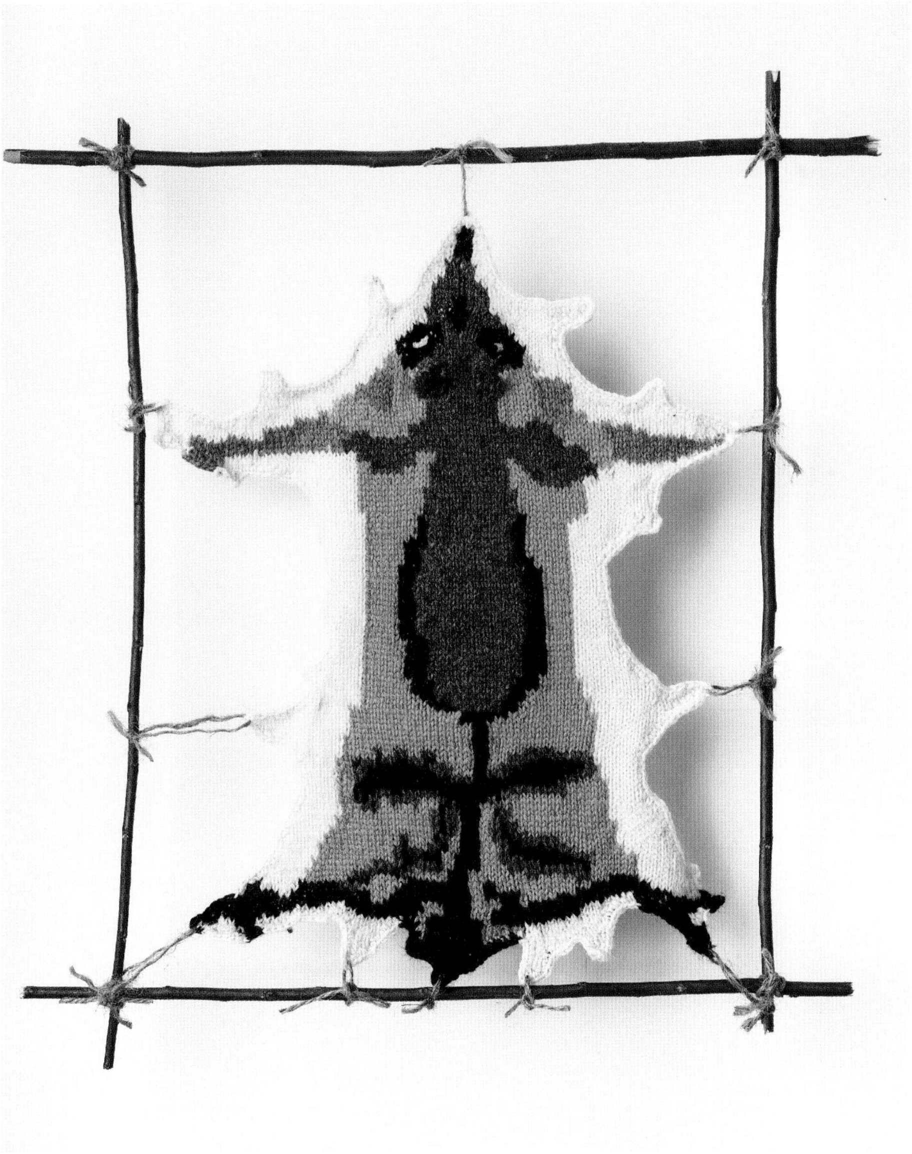

6

5. *Leadbeater's Possum #1*, 2013. An interpretation in yarn of a specimen at Melbourne Museum, Australia.

6. *Bandicoot #1*, 2013, private collection of Bronwyn McCoy and David Marshall.

7

7. Lotus, 2013. Shown at the Brooklyn Botanic Garden's 'Knit, Purl, Sow' exhibition of works by knitting and textile artists exploring the natural world.

Lauren O'Farrell

Lauren O'Farrell's output encompasses all things knit; she is a graffiti artist, author, teacher and leader. She has also been credited with creating the name 'yarn storming' – a milder term than 'yarn bombing' ('bombing and London don't mix well'). Operating under the pseudonym Deadly Knitshade, her graffiti pieces ('knitblasts') have appeared across London, bearing labels with her logo and the word 'whodunnknit'.

Lauren works with the graffiti knitting group Knit the City, who have been operating since 2009. She also cofounded the knitting group Stitch London, which despite its location now has over 10,000 global members, and has become Lauren's full-time job.

Your practice is very diverse. How do you describe your job, and how do you do it all?

My business cards say author and fibre artist if I need to keep it simple. Other titles include Sneaky Stitcher, Woolly Godzilla Wrangler and Giant Knitted Squid Wrestler.

How I do it all is a bit of a mystery to me too. A willingness to give up sleep for what you love, and constant reminders that life should be lived like you may not have long left. Being a cancer survivor helps. You find you want to live like you mean it.

How long have you been knitting, and what inspired you to adopt knit as your medium?

I began knitting in 2005, six months after I began three years of treatment for Hodgkin's lymphoma. I had never knitted before, despite coming from a family of knitters. Friends were relearning, and it was something I hadn't tried before.

Debbie Stoller's Stitch 'n Bitch book was a bit of an inspiration. It showed knitting in a new light – fun, creative and meditative. I knitted very badly for quite a while but I loved it.

Does your environment have an effect on your work?

My street art is highly influenced by where it is created for – the stories and history of a place mean that you're twisting a bit of the world into your work. I rarely make something for the sake of it. There has to be some kind of tale behind it.

How do you start a project, and how do you progress it?

I usually start work with a place in mind. In the case of pieces such as my wildflowers, which are random and made in advance without a place in mind, I choose a place where they will make an impact and get noticed. I tend to go for bright colours that stand out and try to think outside the box when it comes to creating a piece. If you're going to make street art it has to have a story, or give a nod to its surroundings.

Which stitches, yarns and materials do you favour?

I usually plump for eye-popping neon yarns (Cygnet Yarns do a great range of pinks, yellows and greens) because they stand out and remind me a bit of the spray-can street art of the 80s and 90s. Stitchwise, the simpler the better.

As for materials, I use anything I can get my hands on: wire, LEDs, glow-in-the-dark paint, buttons, safety eyes, recycled padded envelopes, sponges. The list could go on. I tend to think of myself as a graffiti crafter rather than just a knitter. My current favourite combo is knitted cord and wire.

Your work invites social commentary. Have you had any interesting experiences relating to this?

I never install anything at night. The process of settling a piece into its place needs daylight, and it's always interesting to interact with people passing by, who either think you're crazy or just want to know what on earth you think you're doing.

What do you consider to be your most successful piece of work, and is this also your favourite?

The giant knitted squid gets a lot of attention, but I'd say that the Parliament Square Phone Box Cosy [near London's Houses of Parliament] is the best known. Probably because of the location, which I chose purely because you can see Big Ben in the background, with no thought for the fact that there are more security cameras there than anywhere else in the UK. The sheer gutsiness of where it is seems to draw people to it.

I also made a private commission for Emma Freud and Richard Curtis inside a shepherd's hut. Eight months of hard crafting to knit an indoor forest full of characters from their favourite books and films, with quotes embroidered on fabric leaves. It was my most epic piece and the one I put most of my heart into. Emma said I was a 'force of nature' when it was complete. Best response ever to my art.

What happens to your pieces after they are removed from a site?

All my public pieces are there to be stolen. I tag everything with a 'Confess your theft' label and my website address, although I have only ever had two confessions and I've done over 100 pieces. I like that they go on to have lives I will know nothing about. I also do my own photography, so I end up ensuring a little bit of immortality for each piece. They live on online.

157.

1

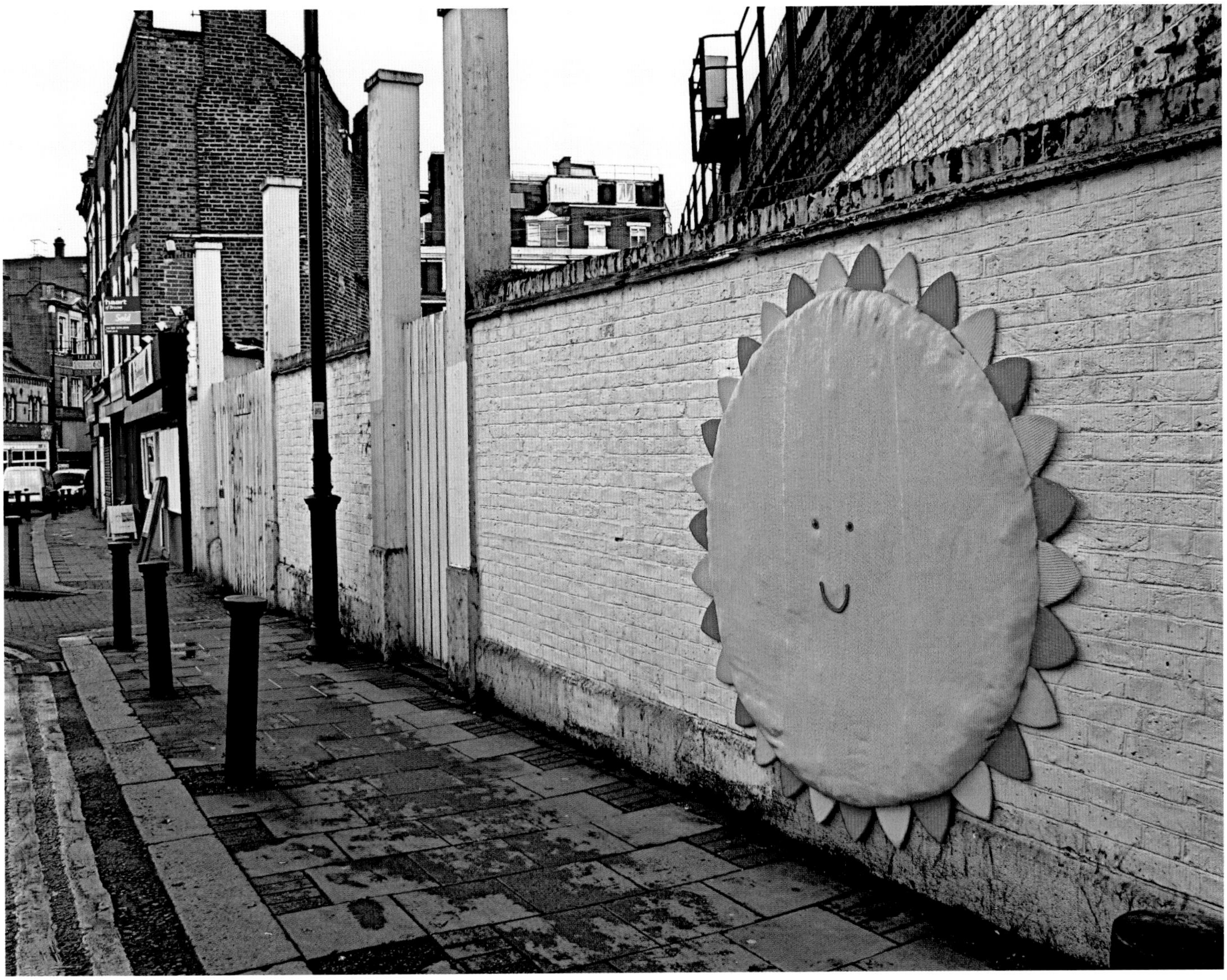

3

1. *Plarchie the Squid*, made from 160 knitted Sainsbury's supermarket carrier bags, makes friends with Charles Darwin at London's Natural History Museum.

2. This delicate wildflower, called *Bloom*, was Knit the City's attempt to brighten up a backstreet in Brixton, bringing an early touch of spring after a long, cold winter.

3. A giant knitted sun, situated on London's famous Brick Lane.

TELEPHONE

5

4. Lauren stands in front of *Dial M for Monster*, created for the 2012 'BT ArtBox' event, in which phone boxes decorated by various contributors were displayed on London streets for a month to mark the 25th anniversary of the NSPCC's ChildLine. Lauren's yellow box was later sold on eBay, raising over £1000 for the charity.

5. The multicoloured, multitextured *Parliament Square Phone Box Cosy* was up for two hours under the shadow of Big Ben before it was removed.

6

6. *Stitched Story Trees*, a private commission for Emma Freud and Richard Curtis, consists of 122 hand-made pieces, including knitted characters from Freud's and Curtis's favourite books and quotes embroidered on fabric leaves.

7

8

7. A knitted pirate hangs precariously from a noose in a pirate castle venue in London's Camden.

8. This knitted homage to Banksy, in the form of a rat holding up a Knit the City sign, was installed in London's Deptford Market as part of Lauren's 'Stitched Street Art Heroes' tribute. Other exhibits in the same series were called *Invader* and *Stik*.

Na'ama Rietti

Working under the name Namarietti, Na'ama Rietti is a 'hybrid' knitwear specialist, creating intricately detailed, exclusive apparel which she defines as 'artwear' – truly original, her work bridges the boundary between art and fashion through a unique and extraordinary aesthetic.

Heavily influenced by her mixed heritage – Mediterranean and Middle-Eastern Jewish of Iraqi, English, Russian and Italian descent – Rietti combines rare and exotic materials with meticulous handcrafting techniques to embody multicultural themes, often evoking a strong sense of spirituality.

How do you define yourself?

Hmm ... I would like to say I am an artisanal designer. I'm not interested in fashion as such; I use knitwear techniques to express and materialize my ideas into wearable art forms. Fashion provides an exciting platform within the creative industry that allows me to successfully utilize my ideas and share my enjoyment in creative expression. If I wasn't on this path, I like to think I'd be exploring philosophy, studying anthropology or travelling to the Moon.

How long have you been knitting, and what inspired you to adopt knit as your medium?

When I was six years old my grandmother taught me to hand-knit; I remember mastering the technique until I could knit with my eyes closed. Encouraged by my mother's never-ending interest in art and creativity, I was always creating something with my hands and eventually directed my creative efforts towards clothing. I discovered knitting machines during my studies at university, where I began experimenting with all sorts of techniques.

How do you start a project, and how do you progress it?

When starting a new project I begin by unearthing a deep focus of interest in my life that inspires me to explore meaning and how these ideas can be interpreted symbolically through texture, shape and colour. I explore ideas through drawing, painting, sculpture, installation and photography; many ideas derive from ambiguous images resembling creatures or bodily forms that seem to emerge from imagery during the creative process.

When challenged to produce my most intricate knitwear sculptures by hand, I relax into a meditative state in order to transform final drawings and ideas into a finished piece.

How would you sum up the aesthetic of your work?

Exotic primordialism.

Who do you imagine your consumer to be?

I'd say definitely some kind of rare, exotic extraterrestrial.

Who or what has inspired you the most?

Exploring the roots of my interests often takes me back to childhood memories, which have had a significant impact on my tastes, values and beliefs. Many of these memories relate to my experiences growing up, travelling in and around Israel and other Mediterranean countries. Encouraged by my parents, I enjoyed a free and somewhat unconventional upbringing; living with the land with little restraint, I was often surrounded by nature's unlimited fascinations and beauty.

Which stitches and yarns do you favour?

I give particular attention to the softness and quality of materials, and with a seemingly innate love of all things luxurious I often use pure hand-spun silk yarns. I particularly love to create contrasts in texture and enjoy combining techniques; this may involve both hand and machine knitting, but mostly I create shapes and forms by sculpting by hand directly on a mannequin or template, twisting, plaiting, knotting and wrapping yarns to create intricately detailed items which are impossible to replicate, rendering them unique.

What other materials do you use – are you tempted to broaden the range?

I love to explore new and exotic materials, which I can use to interpret and combine my ideas. For my recent collection 'Elements of Creation', I discovered an exotic wood from South America called purpleheart, known by Native Americans for its spiritual and healing properties. I was fascinated to find that after cutting the wood it naturally begins to turn shades of purple when exposed to light.

Do you feel craftsmanship and quality are relevant today?

I think craftsmanship and quality have always been and will always be relevant. As much as we may allow ourselves to be consumed and misled by inevitable developments and changes in our cultural systems and environment, craftsmanship and quality are relevant in all aspects of our daily lives, and are what we strive for in all forms of true creativity, innovation and development.

165.

1

3

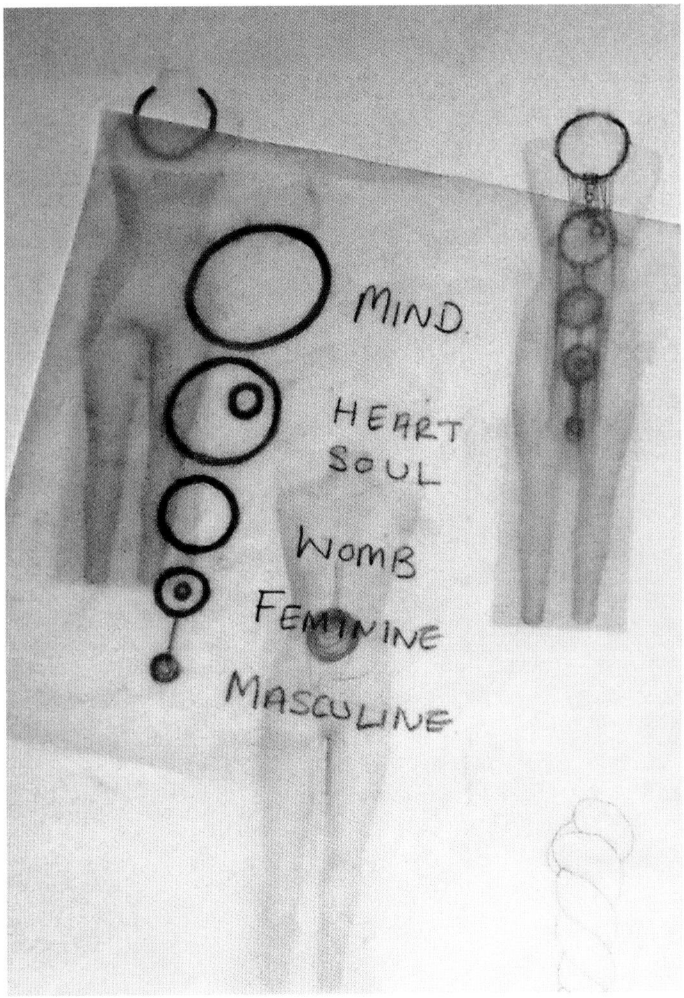

4

1, 2, 3. These jewellery pieces are from Na'ama's 'Elements of Creation' collection, and are made from luxury materials – hoops made from purpleheart wood, adorned with natural or soft pink handspun Indian silk tassles.

4. Na'ama often takes inspiration from her cultural heritage, and explores ideals around identity. The jewellery collection featured on these pages was inspired by 'six elements of creation' – mind, heart, soul, womb, feminine and masculine.

6

5, 6. These ornamental accessories are also from the 'Elements of Creation' collection. As with the pieces featured on previous pages, these combine purpleheart wood with handspun silk, demonstrating Na'ama's love of mixing materials.

7

7. A mood board showing the inspiration behind the 'Animal' clothing and accessories collection. Hair braiding was used to inform the knitted structures of the finished pieces.

8. An installation, alongside some of the objects that inspired it.

9. A model strikes a suitable pose in one of Na'ama's pure silk handspun body accessories, or 'silk sculptures'.

8

9

Magda Sayeg

Credited as the mother of yarn bombing (which can loosely be defined as impermanent graffiti artworks), Magda Sayeg's work has influenced and inspired a generation of graffiti knitters to go out and create. Her work has evolved into a solo pursuit – innovative in her approach, projects include working with corporate companies (Absolut Vodka, Madewell, Mini Cooper), art exhibitions, large installations and community projects. Identifying as an artist, a collaborative worker, a teacher and an activist, she constantly challenges herself and the environment around her.

How do you define yourself?

I don't in general like to identify myself; putting myself in a category leads people to believe there are certain goals that I have. Sure I'm an artist, but did I ever see myself going into a gallery? No. I'm a graffiti artist, but did I have goals to get arrested or pick up a spray can? No. Things that happened to me, there was no precedent for it, there was no name for it. I still don't have a name for it when I think about textile artists. I think about ladies who travel to weird indigenous parts of the world, and that's just not me.

I have taken a traditional craft and transcended the ordinary – that's the easiest way to explain what I do. Sometimes there are political messages to what I do, but not always. Sometimes I just love seeing the knitting on a large scale and in a different environment.

Hand knit or machine knit?

Personally I hand-knit. My labour of love has become a business, so for work I machine-knit; when I have a job I bring in the experts, I bring in the machines. I hand-knit for me.

I always work with the same team. The only way it changes is if I need a larger group of knitters.

Where do you find your colour inspiration?

It comes from everywhere. For example, I recently saw a house ready for demolition; it was built in the 60s and I loved it. I have a colour combination file, and often my colour combinations stem from having one colour that I hate which becomes beautiful when it's surrounded by other purer colours.

Are the team of knitters female?

Yes, predominately female, but there are an increasing number of males participating. Installation is a large part of my work, putting the material on the objects – that brings more men into the picture, as the installation is physical.

I love the installation process. We have so much fun. You see these mundane objects transform into something which is quite beautiful; I think that is an experience we all share together. You don't want it to end, the teamwork is so successful. Community projects reflect the notion that it is not about the individual, it is about the group. To get the ego out of the room can be very challenging.

How do you feel about yarn bombing now?

I have mixed feelings. I see an ugly one and I know there was no direction, no team effort to make one beautiful piece. Some lack direction, lack vision – it can fall short and simply mimic other projects. With good yarn bombing, people have been able to put their egos aside to work on one true collaborative project.

Often it seems to be about quantity rather than quality, and it saddens me that this might be where this movement is going. The corporate world has taken it and wrapped it in a pretty package that is profitable for them. I love it still, but it has been ten years and I am feeling a need to change my approach. I want people to be open to change; all these skilled people, it's a wasted opportunity.

Is anonymity important to yarn bombing?

Honestly, I don't think you have to have anonymity. You can be proud of a project done with one person or with 50 – it's about, I did this with someone, we did this collaboration and this is what happened and the group dynamic wins. With the anonymity that happens on the street there is still an ego involved – it has a signature, it's just that the recognition becomes more underground.

What do you consider your most successful piece of work?

I will always credit the bus in Mexico City as a turning point in my career, as it was my first solo pursuit. When I first started it was a grass roots collective of myself and 12 people; I felt like this was my baby, and the group became just me, although through internal conflict we naturally separated. However the community-led projects that I am invited to direct I equally love – they challenge me in different ways.

My most recent work is evolving. I have been working with Spirographs and ceramics. A friend of mine did this great collection of men with beards and I embellished it – it was so much fun.

Who inspires you the most?

It's an ever-changing world for me, art wise. I love Tom Friedman, Christian Marclay, and Jeff Koons for the supersizing of nostalgic objects. Music, animation, guerrilla gardening in LA – it's all really inspiring ... Aimee Mullins is so incredible ... I love the power of speech. Closer to home, my children teach me so much.

What next?

I am working on a hush-hush project at the moment. I think this might be the crescendo project for me...

173.

1

2

1. A military statue in Bali yarn-bombed by Sayeg in 2010.

2. A street in Milan yarn-bombed in 2008. Sayeg aims to bring softness and human connection into the urban environment with her graffiti knits.

3. This all-terrain vehicle was yarn-bombed in Bali by Sayeg in 2010. For big projects, Sayeg scours thrift stores and garage sales for bright, graphic knits that she can upcycle.

4

5

4. Part of a 2013 installation spanning six floors at New York City's Dover Street Market.

5. Sayeg's 2011 *Knitted Wonderland* installation at the Blanton Museum on the campus of the University of Texas at Austin, USA.

6

6. A roadside picnic in Texas, USA, given the Magda Sayeg treatment in 2012. Playful extremes of scale are evident in the knitted pieces.

7. This bus in Mexico City in 2008 was Sayeg's first solo yarn-bombing piece and a turning point in her career.

8. Sayeg yarn-bombed this street-food cart in Taiwan with a group of local knitters in 2012.

Art: Magda Sayeg

7

8

Annette Streyl

Annette Streyl was born in Munster, Germany. She studied philosophy before embarking on an apprenticeship as a stonemason in 1989; she then studied under acclaimed master sculptors Jan Koblasa and Franz Erhard Walther.

Combining a knowledge of contemporary art and installation, Annette creates knitted architecture, precisely scaled. Her works currently reside in both the public and private domain – pieces are included in the collections of the Kunsthalle in Hamburg, the Deutsches Technikmuseum in Berlin and the Landesmuseum Württemberg, as well as the Falckenberg Collection in Hamburg, where they are displayed alongside avant-garde artists such as Vito Acconci, John Baldessari, Martin Kippenberger, Albert Oehlen, Georg Herold and Daniel Richter.

How long have you been knitting, and what inspired you to adopt knit as your medium?

I started working with knitted architecture in 1998. I had worked on architecture with other materials previously, such as stone or concrete, which led me to wonder which material would contrast with these the most – hence wool.

How do you choose your materials?

I am a sculptor and I do really love working with stone, but in my artwork I try to find suitable materials for the topic I am dealing with. I will approach the subject from different views and therefore use many different materials. I also try to discover something new by using a special or unusual material, and utilizing its properties. Wool is interesting because it does what it wants, not what I want, which leads to more coincidences.

Does your environment have an effect on your work?

I think the environment has an influence on every human being, as well as – or especially – on artists. My focus for a long time was on built surroundings; either being inside architecture or living within cities. Cities grow more and more, and they lack open, free spaces. The built environment is fixed for years, and forces people into certain routes, so I loved the idea of knitted buildings, enabling people to set them aside if they stand in their way.

I think as an artist I feel the same as a non-artist would, someone who is sensitive to this topic – the difference being that I try to find sculptures or pictures to show what I feel.

How do you start a project and how do you progress it?

The most important thing is to find a popular building that is suited to being knitted. I try to choose buildings that represent different fields: for example, a museum represents a cultural position, a bank or a company like IKEA stands for economic power, and the Reichstag for political power.

I then find the construction plans to get all the measurements, as I do all the knitting to a scale of 1:100. If I can't get them, I try to find as many photos and drawings and as much literature as possible about the building, and create my own plans as accurately as I can. I then choose suitable yarns, which represent the special character and show the exact colour of the building. It is often difficult to find all the colours in the same run-length.

Finally, I count and convert all the measurements into rows and stitches. I do this work for my own satisfaction and, of course, in order to exhibit the pieces.

Which stitches and yarns do you favour?

I try to use mostly synthetic yarns, because of moths. If I don't find the correct colours, I use other yarns as well. I focus only on the colour and the surface of a material. I find it difficult to represent glass; for this I use Lurex.

What other materials do you use – are you tempted to broaden the range?

I work with stone, clay and plywood, and I also draw freehand. The choice of materials always depends on the idea, and I try to find the perfect material for it.

Hand-knit or machine-knit?

My work is partly done by hand and partly using a simple knitting machine.

Your work seems to embrace both craft/art and architecture.

Maybe this is because I have a broad education in sculpting. I started as a stonemason; after this, I studied classical sculpture for three years before I went on to study contemporary art/installation.

What do you consider to be your most successful piece of work, and is this also your favourite?

The most successful are the knit works of the Reichstag and the Deutsche Bank. This may be because the Reichstag is the most popular and the Deutsche Bank is very controversial; there are a lot of people who love to see this powerful company hanging like old jeans over a clothesline.

What next for you?

I am actually dreaming of knitting the Kölner Dom (Cologne Cathedral), a famous, huge medieval church. But it might be too complicated.

181.

1

2

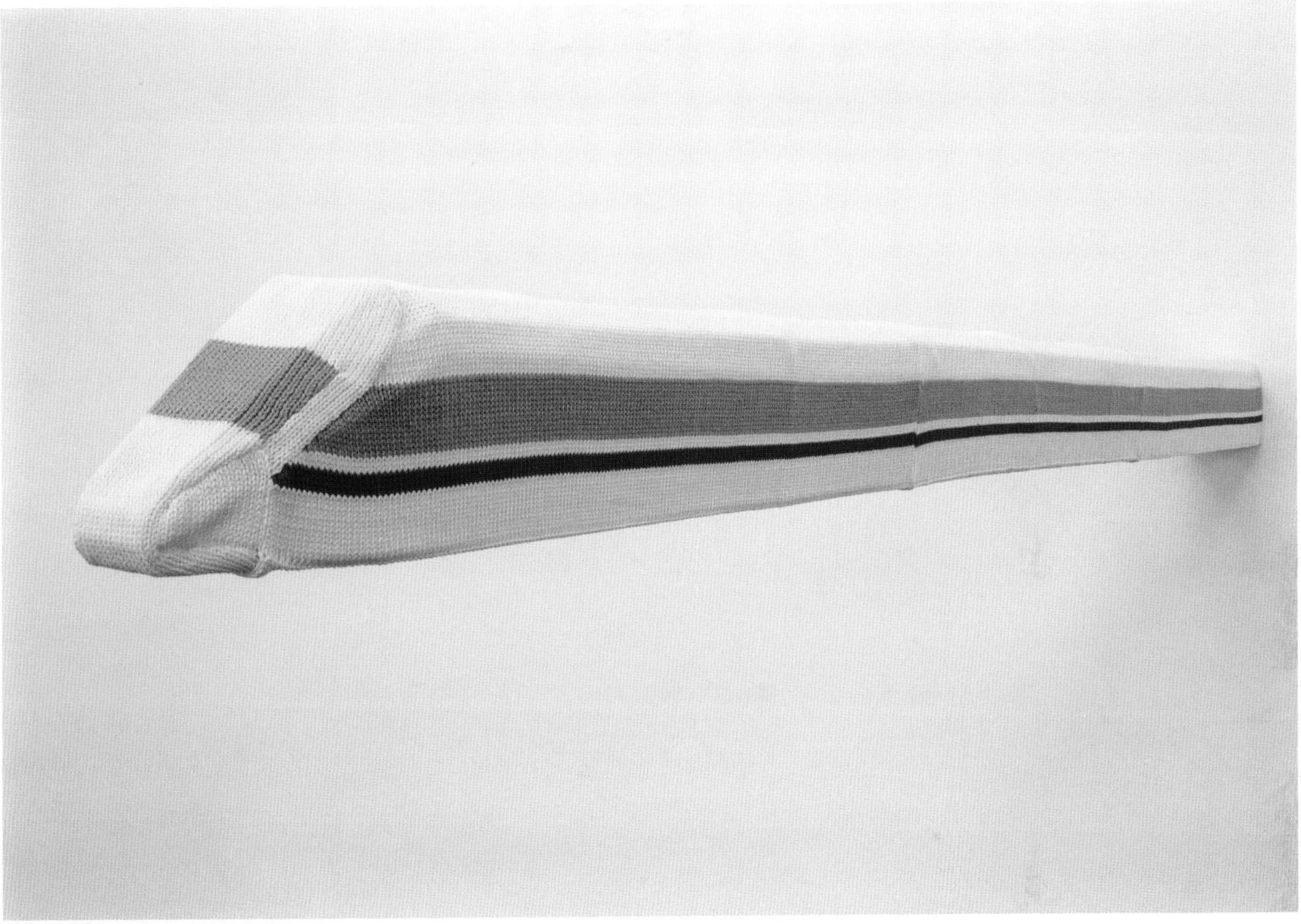

3

1, 2. The two towers of the Deutsche Bank, Frankfurt, captured in wool. The knitted outer skin of Streyl's structure is supported by a frame. The base of the building is suspended a few centimetres above the floor; when the frame is removed, the empty skin resembles an old pair of jeans.

3. Annette is a trained stonemason, and her skills are evident in this dramatic representation of a train, which appears to be driving away from the wall. This train also appears in a collection of knit and stone pieces entitled *Ice*.

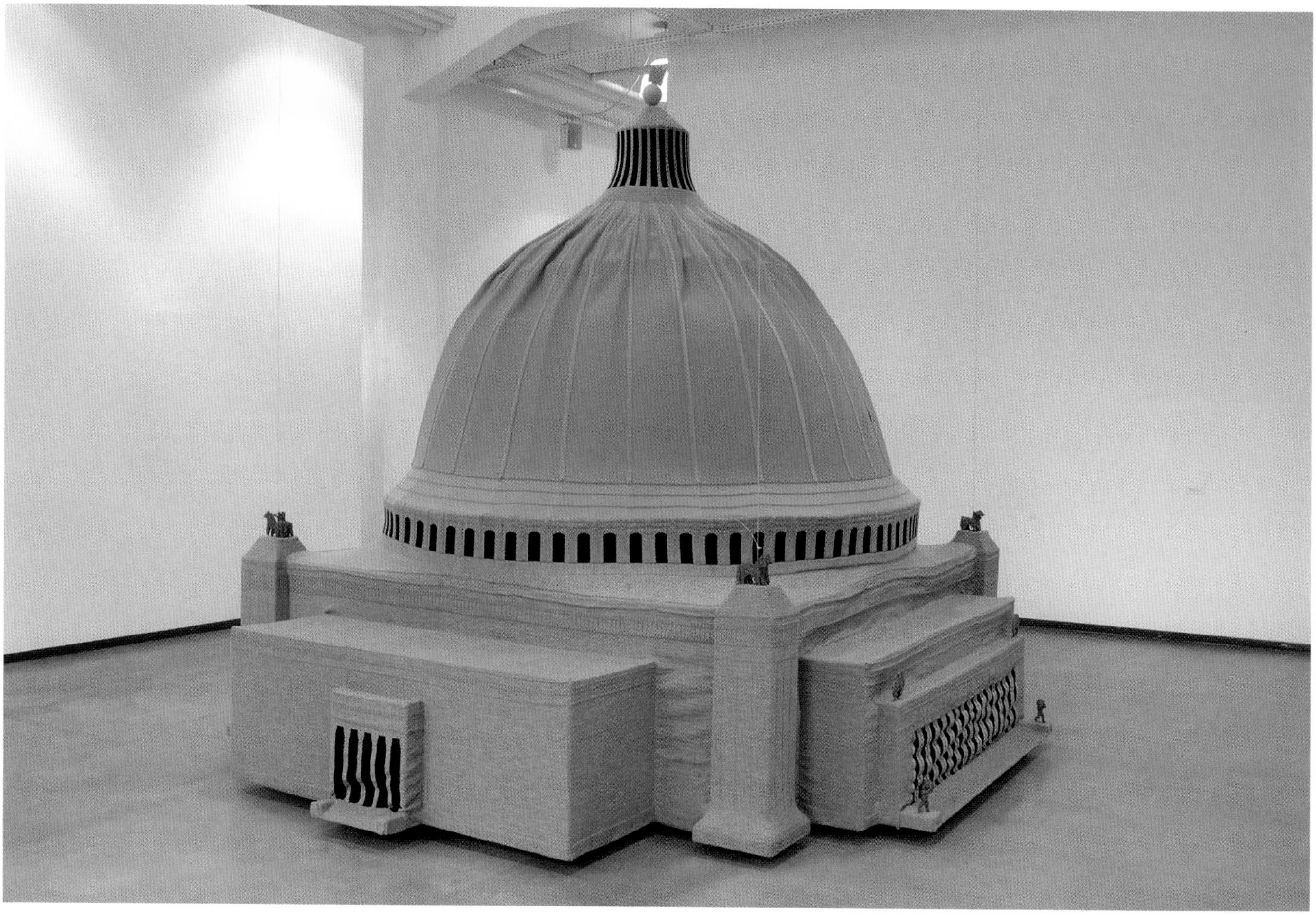

4

5

4, 5, 6. A knitted version of the Great Hall, Berlin, created at a scale of 1:100. Devised by Hitler and his architect, Albert Speer, in 1936, this building was in fact never built.

Art: Annette Streyl

7

7, 8. Streyl's miniature of the Berlin Reichstag captures the symmetry of the original when displayed draped over its frame.

187.

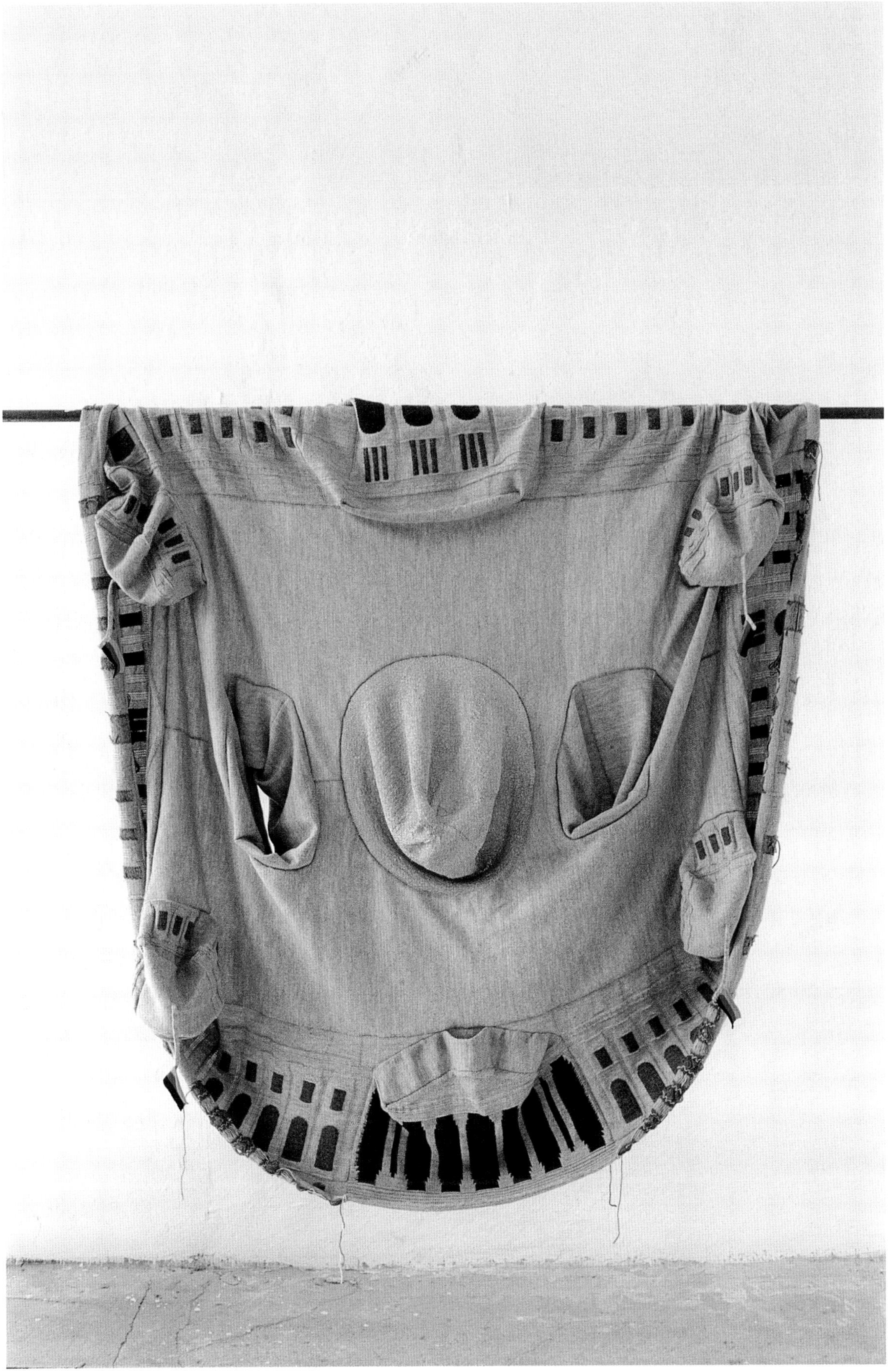

8

Design

The 1980s saw a serious decline in interest in knitting and, correspondingly, the production of yarns and patterns; twenty years later, this trend has reversed, and enthusiasm for the craft continues to grow. The market has responded, and knit has been embraced by designers across many disciplines. Product design and craft practices combine in this section to showcase innovative items and methods of working which reinterpret the knitted structure and represent them to the market in new and exciting ways. Embracing retail, furniture, homewares and community spaces, this section demonstrates the versatility of knit and the vision of the practitioners who choose to push the genre into unfamiliar territories.

Irish knitter Claire-Anne O'Brien collaborates with furniture manufacturers to produce quality items, experimenting with scale and technique to produce innovative bespoke furniture.

Annette Bugansky, an award-winning London-based ceramicist, casts knitted structures using the finest slip, transforming soft textural surfaces into practical, ethereal products, bringing knitting into our home environments in unexpected contexts.

Toshiko Horiuchi MacAdam describes herself as a 'net artist', employing her background as a textile artist to create wonderful, elevated play structures. These demonstrate how honest art pieces, designed from the heart, can be enjoyed by adults and children alike. Placing knit and crochet in an architectural environment, Toshiko's pieces allow access for all, enabling healthier and more joyous community spaces, replacing tarmac and concrete with colour and large-scale constructions.

Catherine Tough is from a family of knitters. Her home products are trailblazers for English knitted goods and are stocked in stores around the world. She has developed a gift market for knitted items, with her nostalgic designs evoking a mood of times past while retaining a contemporary freshness.

Historically, knitters have always worked in groups, with the activity being linked to health and social benefits; a renewed interest in the craft and the reintroduction of the yarn store onto the high street offers an opportunity for retail to promote and embrace these advantages. Spinners are experiencing increased sales and new blends of yarns (as seen at Pitti Filati, a major yarn fair hosted in Florence twice a year) and are feeding the appetites of both new and experienced knitters. In New York, the Yarn Company offers an innovative and unique retail environment, running classes, hosting guest speakers, and bringing to the market artisan yarns and knit design kits, all in a clean modern environment that challenges the perception of the traditional yarn store and haberdashery.

Annette Bugansky

Annette Bugansky graduated in 2005 with an MA in ceramics from London's Central Saint Martins. She combines a background in fashion and costume design with a nostalgic love of knitted fabric and skilled slip casting techniques to transform soft, tactile surfaces into usable vases, lights, cups and sculptural pieces. Annette was awarded the prize for Best New Product (Home) at London's Pulse 2013 for a series of lamps and lampshades, and her original, highly desirable pieces are now sold in a number of European cities.

How do you define yourself?

As a ceramic designer I create designs for tableware, lighting, giftware and sculpture. As well as undertaking all aspects of the making process, from model making, mould making, slip casting and glazing, I also knit, crochet and embroider the textures used for surface decoration.

What is a typical day's work for you?

No two days are the same. When the design and selection of surface and materials is done, production begins. Creating the surfaces is done outside of studio time, often in the evenings and on bus and train journeys. On a typical day I may slip cast up to 20 products in the morning, and make the mould for a new piece in the afternoon. Another day could involve fettling (hand finishing and cleaning) and packing the kiln. The next day the kiln will be unpacked, the products glazed and the kiln re-packed.

There is also admin work – meetings with clients, ordering materials, packing orders, sampling and testing. Then there is research, preparing for shows, marketing, selling, teaching and networking, and commissions for small companies or exhibitions.

Which products do you find to be the most popular?

The knit texture collection. The cups are available in five patterns, the Cable being the most popular; people relate to the cable stitch pattern more than any other. T-lights share equal popularity, with three shapes to choose from, and two patterns to each shape.

Of the vase range, the Interlock is the most popular, featuring a slightly chunkier and complex pattern. The Slub and Pintuck vases, which have been around since the start of the collection, are popular with collectors.

Your work explores the differences between two very contrasting surfaces. What drives you to take a soft fabric and transform it into a hard surface?

My work in ceramics has evolved from my earlier career in fashion and costume design. When I returned to education in 1999 I had planned to study textiles, but I found another material that really excited me instead – clay. In its plastic state, clay is soft and supple, but when fired it becomes hard and strong.

Why do you use knit as a pattern for your ceramics?

Although I also use other surfaces for my ceramics, my love of traditional crafts, textiles, architectural details, types of joins, and connecting, entwining and geometric patterns are ultimately captured in knitting.

How do you start a project, and how do you progress it?

The forms evolve from each other, and many of the curves interlock with each other. This is not always immediately apparent to the viewer. I have a holistic approach to my design process; I am continually producing experimental surface patterns and forms, and function, form and surface all inform each other. I rarely design in 2D except when I am working on technical drawings.

You are a very hands-on maker. How do you cope with large orders, and have you any plans to collaborate with producers?

Long lead times allow me to make everything myself. I organize my time, and bring in people to help with some of the basic jobs, such as preparing clay, rubbing down and packing.

I would love to collaborate with producers and have recently visited factories in Stoke-on-Trent to gain a deeper understanding of factory process, but I still feel factories cannot provide the quality inherent in handmade work. This is something that I would have to accept if I explored this pathway in the future.

Who or what inspires you the most?

Texture, depth, beauty and elegance, whether natural, architectural or man-made. I love entwined patterns and fine details – unfussy, classic, simple, fresh, traditional; anything that looks 'unworked'.

My favourite artists include M. C. Escher, Klimt, Dalí, Petr Weigl and Nick Lee, and the photographers David Bailey, Norman Parkinson and Man Ray.

What next for you?

My most exciting project has been my Fossilized Fashion range, a culmination of my experiences as a designer of both fashion and ceramics. It is an ongoing project that will evolve with time. Otherwise I am planning sculptural, experimental work, exploration of new materials, collaborations with manufacturers.

191.

1

2

3

1. Bamboo pattern vase with flowers. Bugansky's designs capture the texture of knit in handcrafted porcelain.

2, 3. Slub vase.

4. Azalia vase.

Design: Annette Bugansky

4

6

5. Knit and Embellish pendant lights.

6. Diamond and Rib T-lights.

196. Design: Annette Bugansky

Design: Annette Bugansky

8

9

10

7. Stitch pattern jug.

8, 9. Bugansky at work: making adjustments to the surface of a piece before the ceramic is fired and attaching knit texture pieces to a form.

10. In a further exploration of textiles and texture, Bugansky created these small bowls from hand-sewn sections of milliner's wool felt dipped into liquid clay.

Toshiko Horiuchi MacAdam

Toshiko Horiuchi MacAdam trained at the Tama Fine Art University in Tokyo, and then attended Cranbrook Academy of Art in Michigan. After graduating she worked as a textile designer in New York. Toshiko has taught at numerous colleges and universities, and is the author of the two-volume book *From a Line*, which references textile structure work.

A highly regarded textile artist in Japan in the 1970s, Toshiko realized that she wanted to make works designed for children's play rather than for exhibition in galleries and museums. Her first high-profile playspace was created in 1979 and housed at Okinawa Memorial National Park, followed by *Knitted Wonder Space* at the Hakone Open-Air Museum. With her husband Charles MacAdam, Toshiko established Interplay Design and Manufacturing in 1990, creating and promoting art and play for children in national parks. Toshiko is currently working on pieces to be installed in the USA and Canada, where she is now based.

How do you define yourself?

As an artist, I don't think it's important for me to be categorized; it seems to be more important for other people. I create something which is completely new. From the start, having a questioning nature, I was inspired to find the answers to: 'What does it mean to apply surface design to textiles?' and, at its most basic, 'What is a textile?'

Structure and surface, combined, giving equal importance to form and function – this is really important for me, and defines my work.

Your early pieces were restricted by costs. Was limitation the mother of invention? How did you stay motivated?

My pieces were funded by freelance work. I had to work to a budget and there were design limitations due to this; I had to keep the design inexpensive. Initially I designed three pieces, and created the largest one. The geometric crochet came to life when the children played on it – it became a performance piece and it touched my heart. This feeling has stayed with me and drives me forward.

Can there ever be a retrospective of your work?

The pieces themselves get worn; we repair them and maintain them, but they eventually expire. But we work with photographer Masaki Koizumi. The children really love him – he gets on the nets with them and plays. He is from a sports photography background and is able to capture the motion and the movement. Maybe there could be an exhibition of his photographs.

You use crochet in your pieces. Why?

Knots and crochet create a very strong structure, enabling movement and stretch. The weak points are where the nets join the supporting structures and where the structures meet the ground, not in the textile itself.

How does your creative process work?

I keep specific records of each project, how much yarn is used, and construction techniques – these can be referred to. We build maquettes, use CAD, visit sites and have meetings with architects and planners. It is a very collaborative process.

Your pieces are very colourful. What inspires you?

I visit the site and look at the environment and the atmosphere. I may be inspired by the sky, by the landscape. I have textile training and colour was always very important to me; this continues to feed into my work. There are some practical issues too – I tend to use intense colours outside as they are more resistant to UV rays.

Your structures were initially informed by thorough research of children's play. What drives you to dedicate yourself so intensely?

My father and grandfather were doctors and I expected to follow in this tradition, but art took over for me. I am fascinated by children's play and the intense feeling they get from the nets. My brother is a paediatrician, specializing in premature babies. We have discussed parallels between a 'kangaroo' theory that he has been exploring, where a baby is rocked and held skin to skin to mimic being in the womb, and my nets, which also follow this motion. Playing children feed off each other's energy; they rock and you can sometimes see them going into an almost trance-like state. The girls seem to play in a very repetitive way, and the boys, they are all over the place.

It is important to me to keep learning. I am part scientist, part artist, part creative. In my family, although we are coming from different directions, we are heading towards the same goal – health, wellbeing and joy.

How important is collaboration to you?

All my projects are hugely collaborative. Each one is engineered by Norihide Imagawa; he is an architect and an amazing designer, but he is an artist at heart – we are like-minded. He is very supportive and understands the issues we have working with textiles, and works around us. He has supported us and helped me present to government.

We collaborate with photographers, architects, friends, and I have a very supportive network. We work together, and it's great!

1

2

1. MacAdam in her studio, piecing together crocheted sections of an installation.

2, 3, 4. *Harmonic Motion*, a work by Toshiko Horiuchi MacAdam and Charles MacAdam with Interplay Design & Manufacturing, Inc., wth structural design by Norihide Imagawa with T.I.S. & Partners, Co. Ltd.; 2013 Edition of Enel Contemporanea at MACRO Museo d'Arte Contemporanea Roma, December 2013–January 2015.

Design: Toshiko Horiuchi MacAdam

3

4

6

5. An interior shot of the *Hakone Forest Net*, housed in Japan's Hakone Open-Air Museum. Particularly striking is the quality of light entering through the external wooden structure.

6. The exterior of the *Hakone Forest Net*. Installed in Japan's first open-air art museum, this again demonstrates the successful collaborative nature of Toshiko's work. The net design and construction was by Toshiko, with Interplay Design & Manufacturing, Inc.; structural design was by Norihide Imagawa T.I.S. & Partners, Co. Ltd.; project design was by Takaharu and Yui Tezuka, Tezuka Architects.

204. Design: Toshiko Horiuchi MacAdam

7

8

9

7. In this shot of a *T'bob* structure housed in the playground of a public elementary school and kindergarten, it is easy to see the importance of the supporting posts. According to Toshiko, the points where the supports meet the fabric structure are the weakest point of any installation.

8, 9. Details of the *Takino Rainbow Nest*, installed in Japan's Takino Suzuran National Park. Looking up from underneath the structure reveals the detailed joins and the movement of the constructed fibres.

Claire-Anne O'Brien

Originally from County Cork in Ireland, Claire-Anne O'Brien graduated with a degree in textiles from London's Central Saint Martins in 2006, then completed a master's degree in textiles at the Royal College of Art in 2010. In 2011 she set up her East London studio, specializing in constructed textiles.

Claire-Anne has exhibited at the London Design Festival, Milan Furniture Fair, Wool Modern and Spinexpo, and she received a Future Makers Award in 2011 from the Crafts Council of Ireland. Her studio works on private and commercial commissions, and is committed to working with natural materials and local artisans, including a team of loyal hand-knitters.

How do you define yourself?

I would define myself as a textile designer. Though I have been working with furniture, my skills and passion lie in material and fabric development.

What is your role within the company?

There is a lot of preparation involved in a project, such as liaising with clients, sourcing and ordering materials, sampling fabrics, making technical drawings and patterns, and of course knitting. On a daily basis there is always a lot of admin too – arranging press loans, couriers, answering enquiries. As a result there's not as much time to design and experiment as I'd like, so whenever I get a chance I research new materials, markets and trends, and sample ideas for new work.
This is what it's all about!

Which products do you find to be the most popular?

The Knit stools have been the most popular so far – in mustard and blue.

Your work explores scale and the knitted stitch. What inspires you?

I immerse myself in materials, surface and colour. I also take lots of photographs, collect fabrics, colours and materials, and I scour the internet. At the moment I am particularly interested in traditional techniques such as rug making, weaving and knotting, so I have been doing a lot of research into those.

Ultimately it is the material that inspires me the most, so it's through playing with materials and investigating different construction techniques that I am most inspired.

How do you manage production? Is collaboration important to you?

Production has been the biggest challenge by far and has only been resolved through trial and error. I've had to learn about new processes such as carpentry and upholstery, and I now have reliable suppliers to make the furniture and to upholster. It's taken time but it's crucial to have good relationships with suppliers you trust to deliver high-quality work.

I still handle a lot of the production myself, but I now also outsource certain parts. The Knit stools have recently been licensed to Gandia Blasco, a large rug and furniture manufacturer, which is exciting; they will produce the stools and develop the range much more than I could.

I am also currently working on a fashion collaboration with Natalie Coleman. I started out in fashion so it's nice to be revisiting it.

How long have you been knitting, and what inspired you to start?

I learnt to knit in primary school – we made sweaters for teddies, which I still have! But it was not until I did a fashion design course that I rediscovered knitting, and transferred to a textiles course.

How do you start a project, and how do you progress it?

It depends on the brief – if it's for a client or self-directed. But at the core of my practice is material and technique investigation, so for me the material or yarn always comes first. As a designer and maker, I design through making, where fabric experiments are suggestive of use or application and are developed accordingly.

Can you explain a bit about the UNESCO project you were involved with?

The Royal College of Art and UNESCO invited us to work with the Snow Leopard Conservancy Trust, a small NGO in northern India. They have established various initiatives that supplement local villagers' incomes with the agreement that they will then protect, rather than kill, snow leopards.

Though knitting is not a traditional skill there, the women were already knitting simple socks and hats for themselves. Using local yarns such as sheep and yak, we worked with them to develop products that could be sold to tourists along the trekking routes. We were based in Leh, Ladakh, but travelled to remote villages to live and work with the locals.

We incorporated local motifs into handwarmers, socks and hats. We also made small knitted animals native to the region, such as snow leopards, ibex and sheep. These have been extremely successful and the villagers are now teaching other villages how to make them.

What next for you?

I am working with some Irish spinners to develop interior fabrics using their new 100 per cent Irish wool – it's nice to be working so closely with the source material/manufacturer.
It is important to keep evolving as a designer and so I would also like to focus more on research and material experimentation than on finished products and see where that takes me!

207.

1

Design: Claire-Anne O'Brien

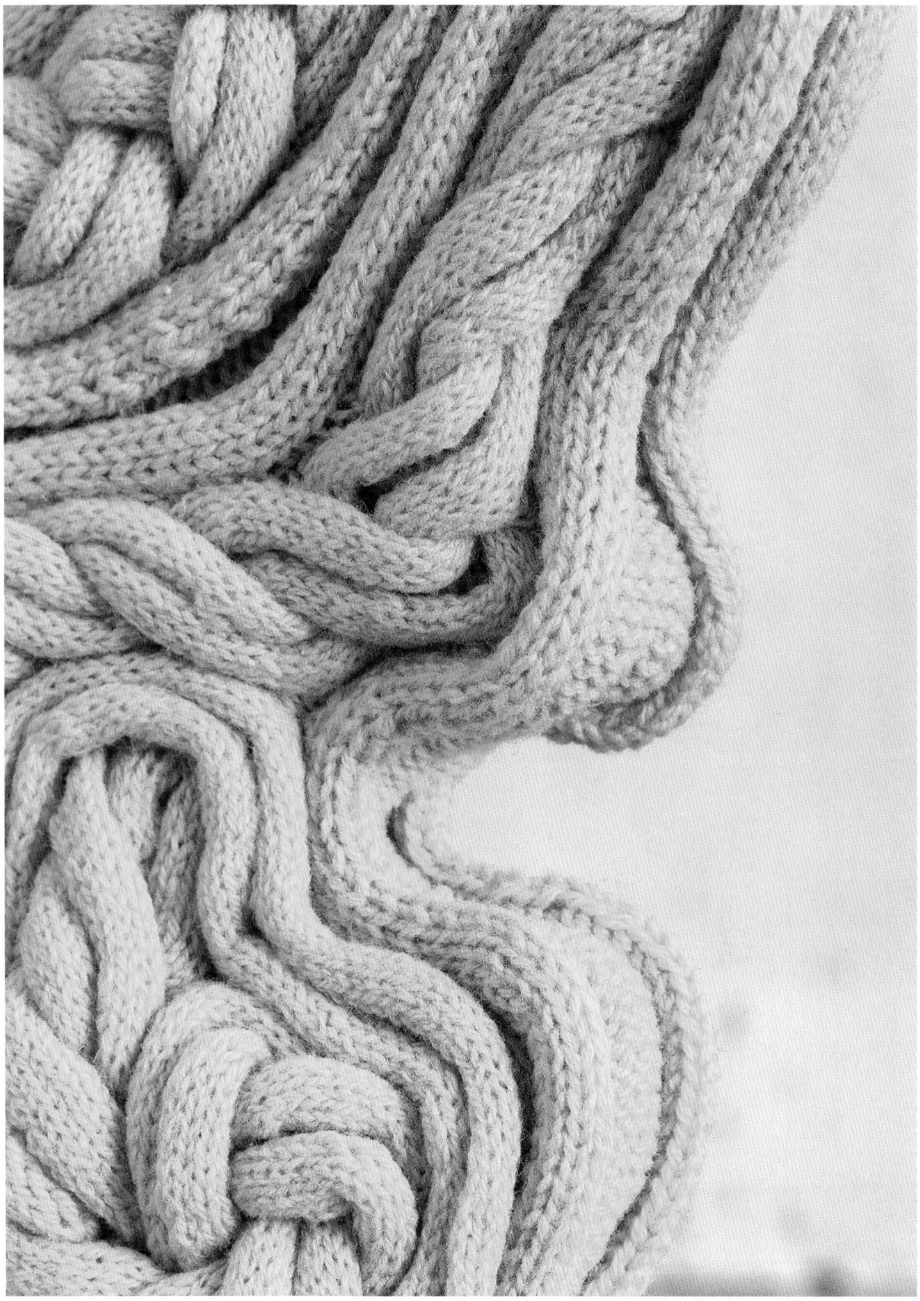

3

1. Knitted tubes are woven over a knitted base, giving the Bainain chair a three-dimensional feel.

2, 3. For the Casta chair, knitted tubes are twisted together and coiled around the seat and back of a wooden frame to create an organic shape.

4

4. For the Fite stool, Laxtons Mill bespoke wool (made at one of the oldest spinners in the UK) is used to create knitted tubes, which are then interlaced to cover a simple footstall with ash legs, updating a classic piece of furniture.

5

6

5. A selection of O'Brien's work materials in the studio – yarn on the reel, knitted sections and strips of knitted tubing.

6. A piece of braided knit before construction.

7, 8. The 'Olann' collection is a series of simple furniture pieces, inspired by the Irish traditions of fishing and knitting, and featuring patterns based on Aran sweaters, fishing knots and willow baskets. (Olann means 'wool' in Irish.) Each item is made entirely by hand using Laxtons Mill wool, with natural materials such as coconut fibres and duck feathers replacing the usual synthetic upholstery materials. Shown here are the Cruinn and Ciséan Beag stools.

Design: Claire-Anne O'Brien

7

8

Catherine Tough

Award-winning Catherine Tough graduated from the Royal College of Art, London, in 1999. She is known for her knitted products, showcasing pattern and colour. A trailblazer for the knitted gift market, Catherine's products and accessories are sold in boutiques and department stores around the world. Catherine is also a respected author and a teacher.

How do you define yourself?

Always a knitter ... director of Catherine Tough Textiles Ltd.

What is your role within the company?

Production is run by our studio manager so I focus on sales, the day-to-day ordering of materials and upkeep of the studio, book-keeping, organizing trade shows, liaising with our PRs, business development, working on the website and developing new products.

Knitting runs in your family (Catherine's sister Clare is a fashion knitwear designer). Why is this?

My mum was always making things when we were small, from duffle coats to batwing dresses – she even had a spinning wheel and collected fleeces. All three of us sisters did creative degrees, which people nevertheless find odd, as our parents both have scientific backgrounds.

You graduated with a degree in knitted textiles. Why did you decide to make products, as opposed to fashion, and how did you learn the skills needed to run a business?

I always made products right through my BA, and made a collection of footstools for my final show. After graduating from the RCA I developed a collection of interiors products, including hottie covers, cushions and throws, which luckily sold well at the first trade show we did.

I have had to learn the business side of things as we've gone along. I started off trying to do everything, but I now believe it is very important to get the best people you can to help out with the bits you struggle with, then life becomes much easier.

What keeps you knitting?

Even after more than ten years I really enjoy the process – developing new products and the business. I have never had a day I didn't want to go into the studio. Since having children it allows me the freedom to work round them, which is great.

Which products do you find to be the most popular?

Our socks and lavender doorstops.

How important to your business is your e-shop?

At the moment our wholesale business is our biggest market, but we are working on building the retail side of things, aiming for a 50/50 split.

How do you start a project, and how do you progress it?

I often have an animal or product in mind, and start experimenting with the shape, which can be tricky to get just right. Then the colour and pattern fall into place.

Do you still get involved in the production, and is it all British-made?

Yes, all of our lavender products, hotties, cushions, hats and scarves are made at the studio in Hackney, East London. When it is really busy I often help out with production. We work with a small manufacturer in Portugal for our socks and throws, and have developed a good relationship with them over the years.

Who has inspired you the most?

My tutors at college, especially Fiona Ross and Freddie Robins, were very influential in pointing me in the direction of product rather than fashion.

What next for you?

Developing a summer range (line), in order to overcome the seasonal associations of wool. We might even try some printing!

215.

1

2

Design: Catherine Tough

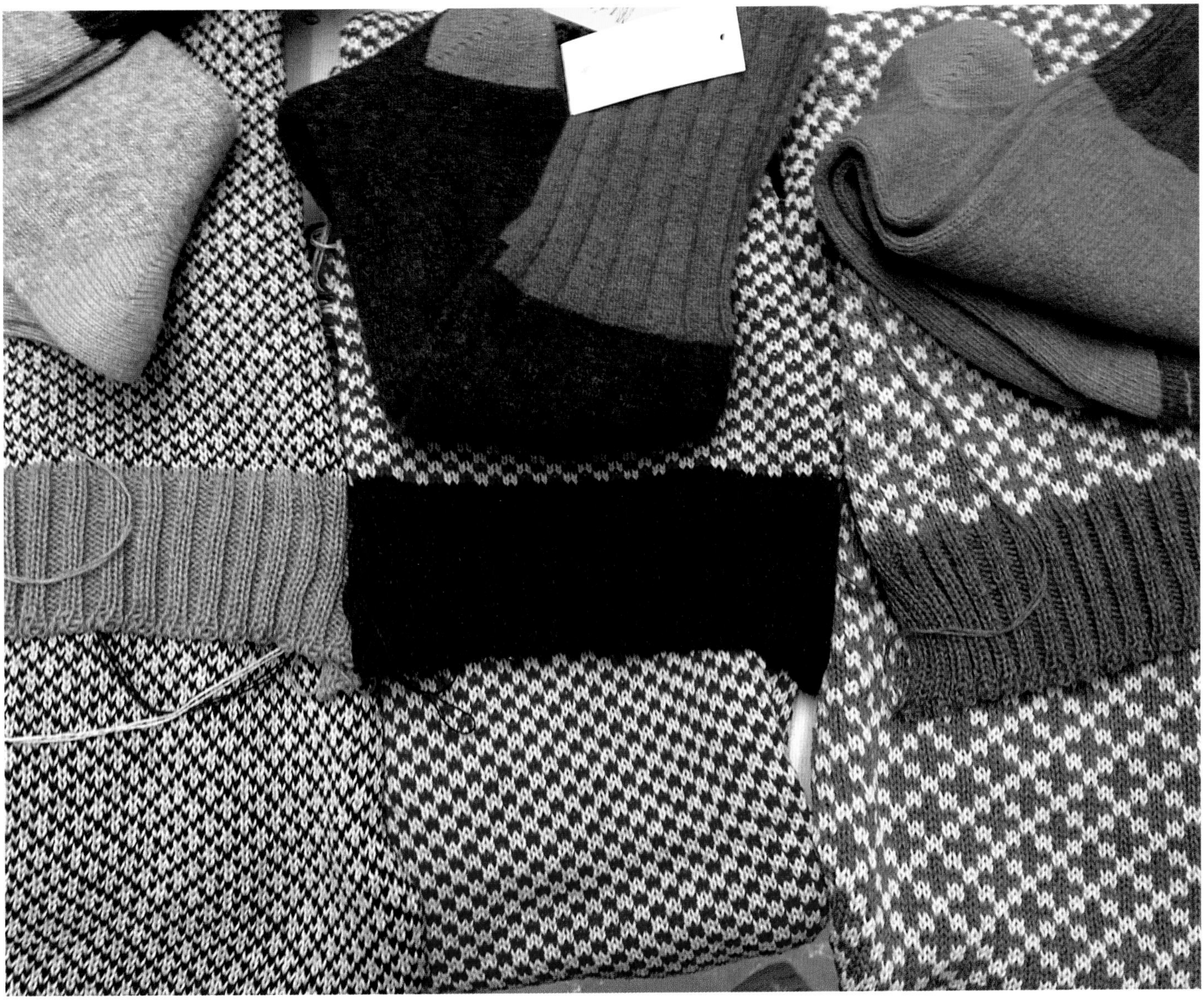

3

1. These knitted lambswool swatches of colourways inspire designs, and also act a selling tool when meeting prospective clients.

2. A variety of yarns and technical swatches, before and after finishing (washing and pressing).

3. Finished and unfinished product. Note the difference in fabric quality between the washed and unwashed pieces. Correctly finished knitted lambswool can demonstrate some of the properties commonly associated with cashmere – a softness to the touch and a discernible fluffiness.

Design: Catherine Tough

4

5

6

Design: Catherine Tough

7

4. These gloves demonstrate clever pattern placement and use of colour blocking.

5. Catherine's studio creates a range of unusual and inventive products, such as this knitted bow-tie brooch.

6. Catherine was one of the first designers to turn a knitted hot water bottle cover into a desirable trend item.

7. These knitted hearts are filled with lavender for encouraging sleep or for imparting a subtle scent to linens and lingerie.

220. Design: Catherine Tough

Design: Catherine Tough

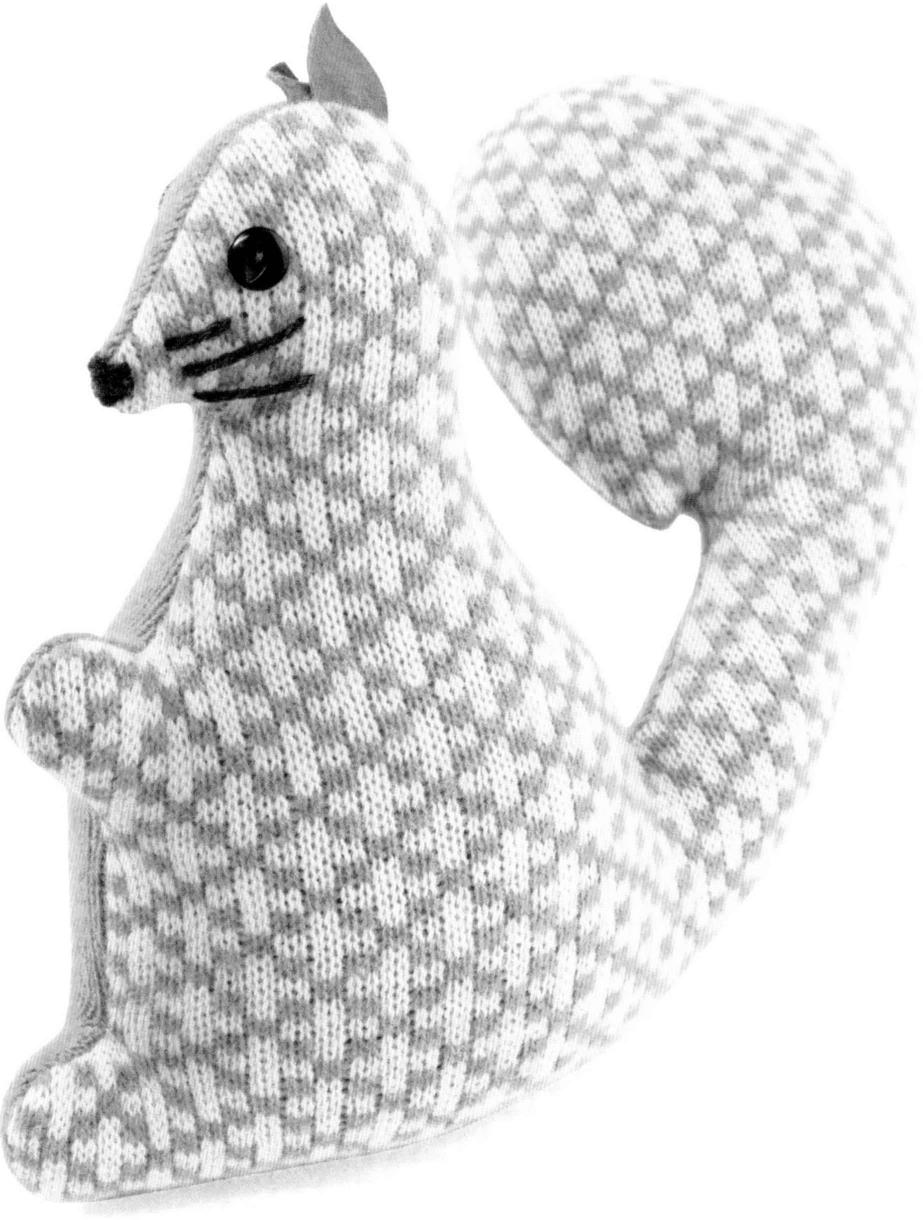

9

8, 9. Catherine produces a wide range of fun characters. Filled with lavender, and gently felted, these knitted toys can also be used as doorstops.

Woolly Thoughts

Husband-and-wife team Pat Ashforth and Steve Plummer are the brains behind Woolly Thoughts, a group on Ravelry, the online knitting community launched in 2007. Ravelry now boasts over 3 million members worldwide, and Woolly Thoughts is one of the largest groups, with over 18,000 members. Both retired maths teachers, Ashforth and Plummer combine mathematical theory with knitting and crochet to create fabrics that explain or depict mathematical ideas, exploring their theory that maths can be accessible through craft. Some of their work could be described as geometric, but you are as likely to find algebra or number theory at the heart of a piece.

Based in the north of England, Ashforth and Plummer work with students and crafters who find mathematics challenging, and their works have been picked up by educational institutions as far afield as New Zealand. In addition to being published authors, Ashforth and Plummer also teach, and some of their work is in the collection of London's Science Museum.

Who belongs to your Ravelry group?

Woolly Thoughts was set up by a fan in 2008 and attracts members who are interested in mathematics and science. We have some high-powered mathematicians and academics, working with complex and highbrow mathematical theories, alongside members who simply regard maths as an interest or hobby, and others still who could be described as maths phobic.

As well as providing an online forum, Ravelry has helped fans of our work to arrange workshop tours and events in England, the USA, Australia and New Zealand.

What attracted you to knitting?

I [Steve] studied maths and art in my teacher training, and people often suggested that this was a strange combination. I am, however, a strong believer in the idea that we should extend our competence over as wide a field as possible. My art was always very linear, almost geometric, and complemented maths. The use of knitting to create mathematical wall hangings to fulfil a need in our maths classrooms seemed a logical extension of this maths/art combination.

More recently, we have turned our attention to illusion or shadow knitting, a style of knitting where you see only stripes when you look directly at the front of a piece, but see an image when you view it at an angle. Our confidence with charts and charting has allowed us to develop the charting process for illusion knitting, which has, in turn, allowed me to create far more complex images than was previously possible.

Tell me a bit about the theory of using knitting to explain mathematics.

Pat and I were both teaching maths in a school with children who did not speak English as a first language; some came to us with no prior formal education – some had never even held a pair of scissors or used a ruler. The large-scale mathematical wall hangings we created provided a colourful and tactile means by which we could, with the help of other children's translation skills, explain mathematical ideas, concepts and vocabulary to these children.

When starting a new work, are you able to visualize the outcome?

Pat and I sit down to discuss ideas; because of the nature of mathematics, within each idea there are hundreds, if not thousands, of potential ideas. We are now very experienced – Pat was knitting without patterns when I met her.

We are sometimes working with experimental maths, developing angles and shapes. We were approached by a client to knit an interpretation of a Peano curve; we had to consult a very old mathematical book to find this. Knitting wasn't appropriate as the curve is a space filler, so Pat used crochet.

What has been your most interesting experience relating to knitting?

One of our methods, whereby students are shown how to knit half-and-half squares (which start from one stitch and increase) was used by the University of Wales, as well as a large number of schools in the UK and abroad. Individual squares are knitted to a template and tension is therefore not important. Every student knits their own square, then all the squares are fitted together to create patterns. Mathematical investigation can then be undertaken by looking at the number of distinct patterns that can be created from two, three, four or more squares.

These students then took this knowledge to local schools and taught it to the children there; the children in turn brought in parents, grandparents and friends to help finish the large afghans they were making with their squares. This was a total success and a wonderful example of community participation. One school noted that the conversations taking place during the class had made a notable difference to a drugs problem that had been occurring; the social interaction and sense of equality fostered by the task was considered a major factor.

1

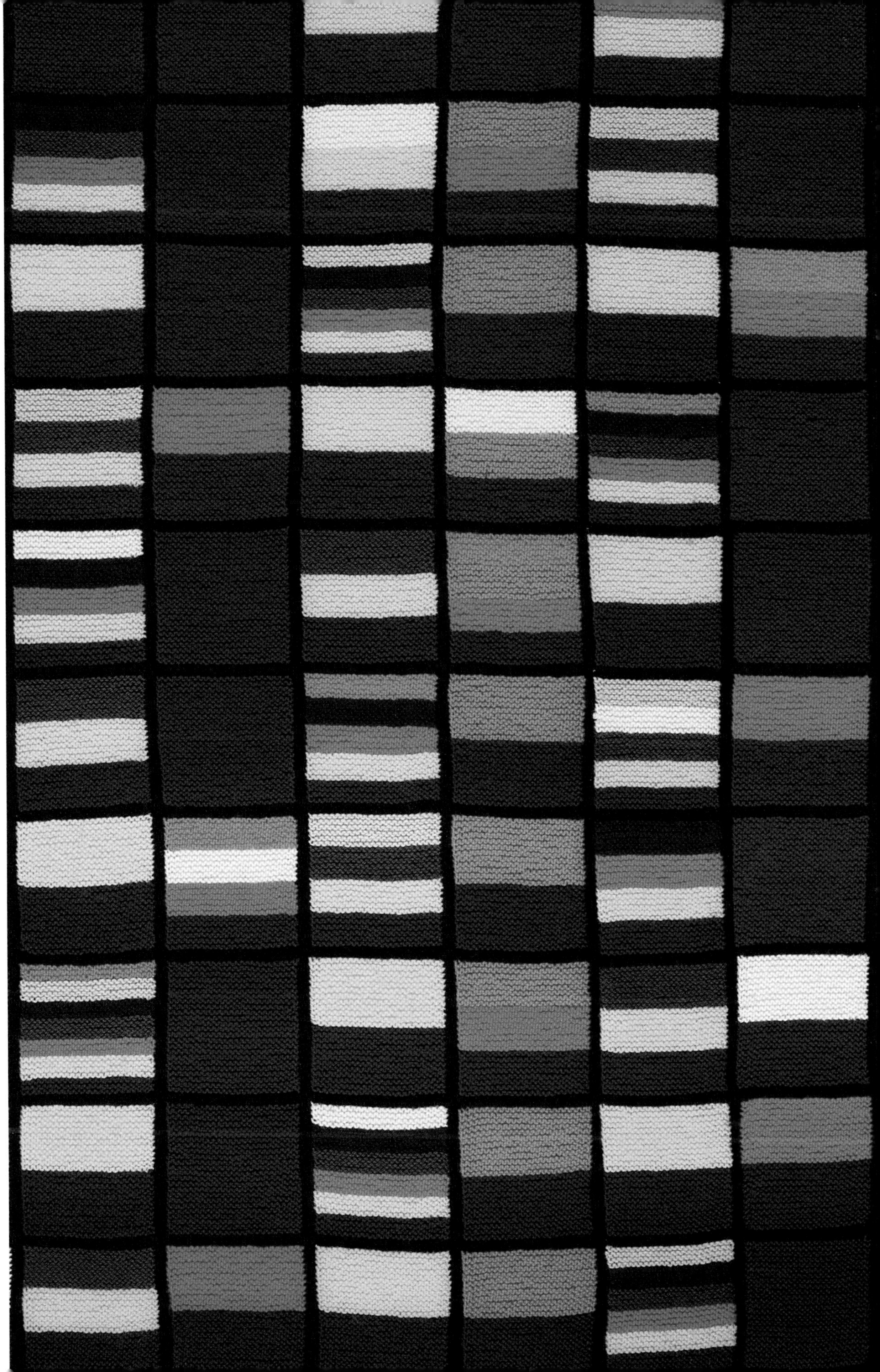

2

1. Counting Pane, a knitted design showing factors 1–10 in numbers up to 100.

2, 3. This Penrose tiling, knitted by Pat Ashforth, is not just a pleasing design with a repeating pattern but an expression of mathematical principles of ratio and symmetry.

225.

3

226.

Design: Woolly Thoughts

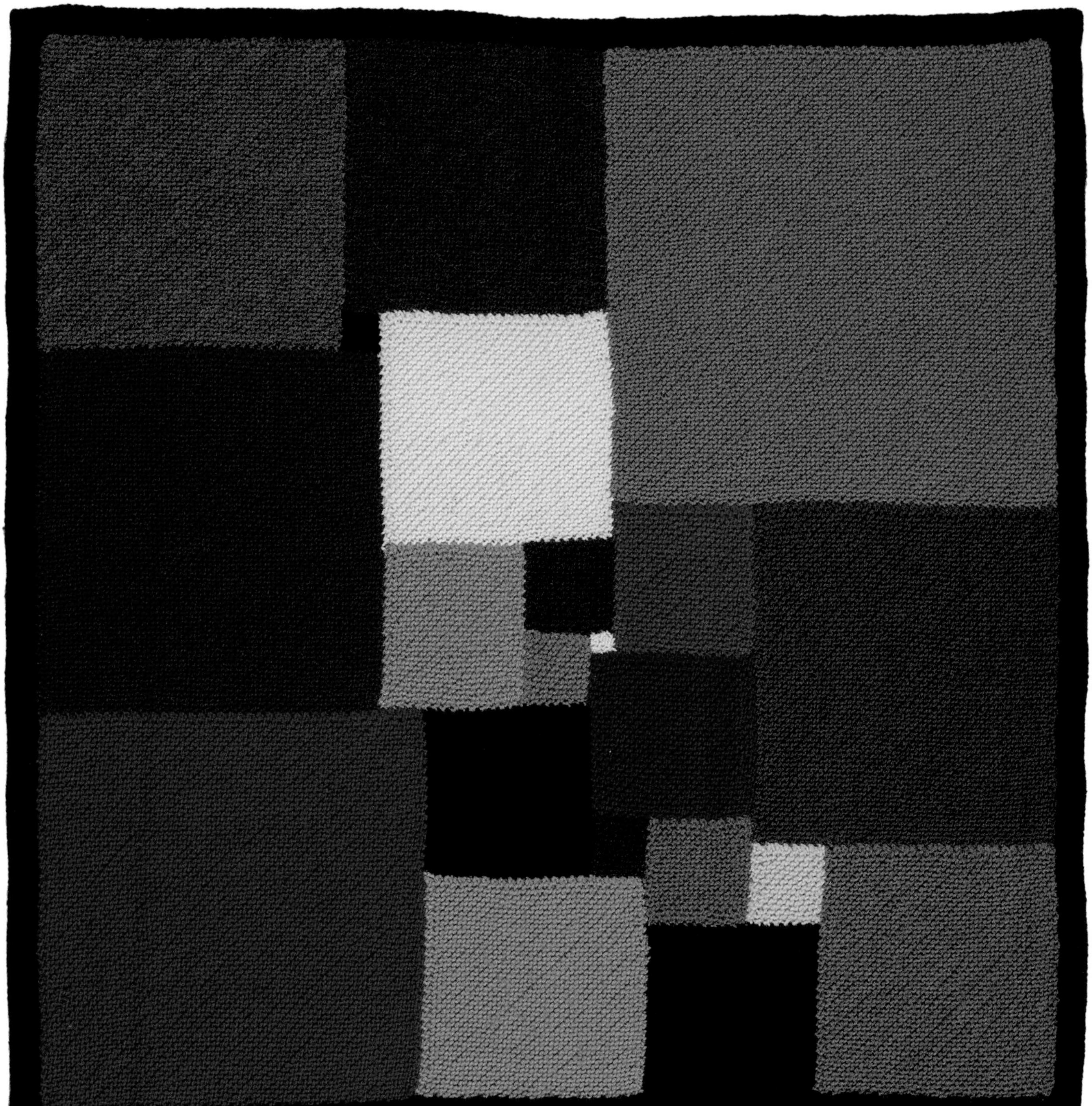

5

6

4. Square Deal demonstrates the minimum number of squares of different sizes in a square.

5, 6. Knitted dominos.

7

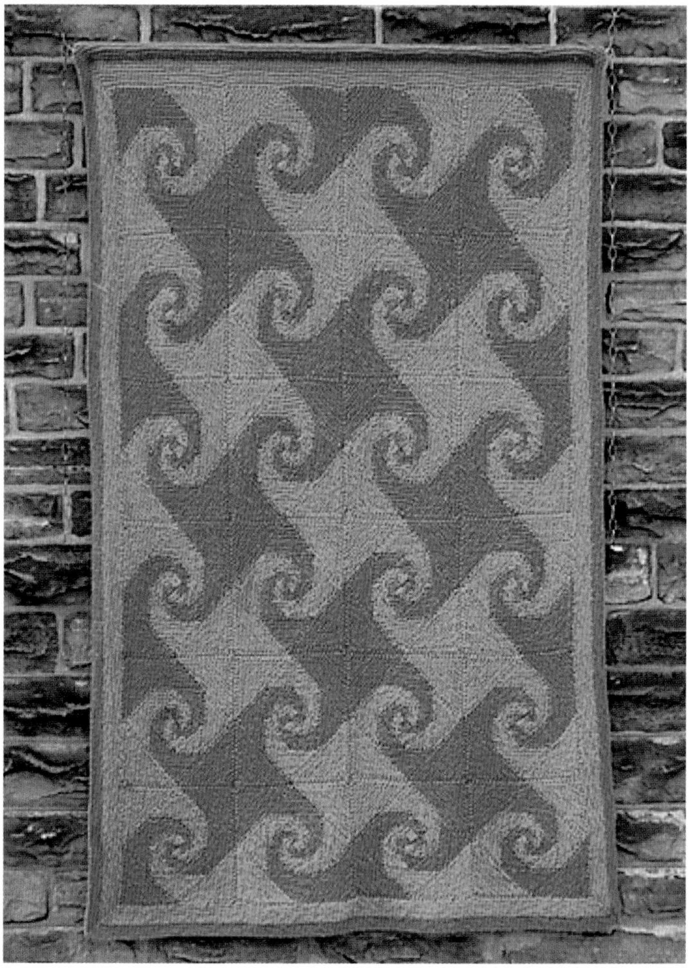

8

7. About Turn afghan, showing one of the thousands of ways that half-and-half squares can be combined.

8. The Best of Both Whirls design looks like it is made up of curves but actually contains only triangles. This afghan consists of 24 identical squares creating Baravelle spirals.

9. Dodecagon Thing knitted blanket, demonstrating a mathematical proof showing how the area of a dodecagon can be doubled to create a larger dodecagon.

229. Design: Woolly Thoughts

The Yarn Company

The Yarn Company stocks a selection of high-quality, hand-dyed yarns and fibres, beautifully presented in a very contemporary way. Rather than offering the usual retail range, their products are generally sourced from festivals or bought direct from artisan makers, and cater for clients looking for something special and a little bit different. Glitzy disco bags are showcased alongside gossamer shawls, knitting kits, patterns and books.

This approach is backed up by the provision of classes and weekend workshops, taught by well-respected practitioners. The Yarn Company has also forged a place for itself as the unofficial spinning centre of New York City. Under the direction of spinning teacher Donna Panner, it plays host to a group known as Spin City. The group meet once a month and have forged a lively knit community in the city, welcoming newcomers of all ages.

Brother and sister Assaf and Tavy Ronen are the owners of the Yarn Company, while Amy Tyszkiewicz is the store manager and a longtime member of Spin City.

How many are there in your Spin City group, and where do you meet?

Our Spin City meet-up spinning group now has approximately 200 members. We meet once a week in various locations in and around New York City.

Who comes to your group?

Spin City counts in its membership men and women from a variety of economic backgrounds, and ranging in age from their 20s to their 60s. The atmosphere is casual, fun and supportive.

The Yarn Company strives to provide a welcoming space for all fibre-related groups, and to provide a selection of the necessary materials and other support for educational purposes.

Do you host events?

The Yarn Company hosts a variety of events, from the aforementioned Spin City group, to trunk shows for books and magazines such as *Vogue Knitting*, to master classes. We host art exhibitions by global practitioners, and receive constant submissions, including work from top design schools. Guest artists from around the world grace the NYC boutique for workshops, events, signings and more. We also host a competition, show at trade shows, work on projects with top designers, have facilities to teach online, and are official sponsors of knitwear design courses at a top textile school in Tel Aviv, Israel.

Monthly clubs, such as the Westknits Shawl Club, feature surprise monthly exclusives for members, and there are regular appearances by top knitterazi and textile knit designers such as Brandon Mably, Kaffe Fassett, Nicky Epstein, Lily Chin, Stephen West, Shirley Paden, and Gryphon Corpus of the Verdant Gryphon. Experts in everything from Icelandic lopi sweaters to mouthwatering lace drop in from around the world at a dizzying rate.

Do you think living in New York has an effect on the design choices your knitters make?

We [Assaf and Tavy] were raised in New York in the 70s and 80s, when it was Punk New York, Hip Hop New York and Indie Film New York. People with the do-it-yourself ethos of these subcultures exploded into art and dance and fashion. We don't really believe that art and craft and fashion are separable. Our customers do not knit or sew or embroider or weave to recreate what they see elsewhere. They do it to express their fashion ideals.

What are your most popular yarns?

Our customers tend to gravitate towards hand-dyed yarns and fibres, especially those that are exclusive to our shop. The Yarn Company takes its customers' aesthetic sense seriously, and supplies the tools for realizing their visions.

Do you also offer classes?

Yes, our think-tank-style classes include weekly and semester-long programmes in everything from the most basic to the most esoteric. These are taught by the Yarn Company's star-studded design staff and hand-picked teaching experts from within the industry.

We also lead the annual 'Knit in Style' workshop weekend, held at the renowned Mohonk Mountain House resort in the Hudson Valley.

What next for you?

Oooh, we have lots of secret projects coming up! Check out our master design classes online, our app that calculates the yarn requirements for pretty much any size of any garment or blanket, and our growing gallery of designer showcase pieces. We are expanding daily – and our machine knitwear classes are garnering much attention.

231.

1

Design: The Yarn Company

2

3

4

1. Glass jars of buttons and fastenings in The Yarn Company shop in New York.

2. Skeins of yarn.

3. Twisted skein of dark blue Midnight in Manhattan yarn, The Yarn Company's exclusive colourway from Madelinetosh.

4. Rubik's Blanket, an exclusive Yarn Company design by Irina Poludnenko.

Capezio

6

5. Midnight in Manhattan sweater designed by Laura Zukaite. The Yarn Company's exclusive design kits give home knitters the patterns and yarns to make their own designer garments.

6. Chameleon Cowl, a Yarn Company exclusive, by designer Irina Poludnenko.

7

7. Neckwarmer in the Yarn Company's exclusive Desert Sand Cashmere, shown in Fifties Formica Green, by designer Irina Poludnenko.

8. Coup de Coeur shawl in the Yarn Company's exclusive colourway Stoplight from Lorna's Laces. A Yarn Company Exclusive by designer Zabeth Loisel-Weiner.

Design: The Yarn Company

8

Designers Directory

Fashion

Alice Lee
www.alicelee.co.uk

Ornella Bignami
Elementi Moda
www.elementimoda.com

Mark Fast
www.markfast.net

Ramón Gurillo
www.ramongurillo.com

John Smedley
www.johnsmedley.com

Leutton Postle
leuttonpostle.com

Markus Lupfer
markuslupfer.com

Irina Shaposhnikova
British Higher School of Art and Design, Moscow
britishdesign.ru

Shima Seiki
www.shimaseiki.com

Sibling
www.siblinglondon.com

Carlo Volpi
www.carlovolpi.co.uk

Christian Wijnants
www.christianwijnants.com

Woolmark
www.woolmark.com

Art

B-Arbeiten
www.ute-lennartz-lembeck.de

Isabel Berglund
www.isabelberglund.dk

Liz Collins
lizcollins.com

Chia-Shan Lee
www.chiashanlee.com

Ruth Marshall
www.ruthmarshall.com

Lauren O'Farrell
www.whodunnknit.com

Na'ama Rietti
namarietti.wordpress.com

Magda Sayeg
www.magdasayeg.com
knitta.com

Annette Streyl
www.streyl.net

Design

Annette Bugansky
www.annettebuganskydesign.com

Toshiko Horiuchi MacAdam
netplayworks.com

Claire-Anne O'Brien
www.claireanneobrien.com

Catherine Tough
www.catherinetough.co.uk

Woolly Thoughts
www.woollythoughts.com

The Yarn Company
www.theyarnco.com

Photo Credits

11–14, 15 (left) Courtesy Alice Lee, A/W Lookbook Campaign 13, Lena C. Emery
15 (right), 16–17 Courtesy Alice Lee, S/S Campaign 14: Photography and set, Lena C. Emery; hair, Fumi Maehara; makeup, Nami Yoshida; model: Katya IMG
19–21, 23–25 Courtesy Ornella Bignami
22 Courtesy Pitti Filati, photo: F. Guazzelli
23 Courtesy Pitti Filati, photo: Claudio Bonoldi Studio
27, 28 (left) Antonio de Moraes Barros Filho/WireImage/Getty Images
28 (right), 29 Rex Features
30–31 Courtesy Mark Fast
32 Stuart C. Wilson/Getty Images
33 Broadimage/Rex Features
35–37 Manuel Queimadelos Alonso/Getty Images
38–41 Catwalking
43–49 Courtesy John Smedley
51–53, 57 Courtesy Leutton Postle, photo: Amy Gwatkin
54–55 Courtesy Leutton Postle, photo: Simon Armstrong
56 Courtesy Leutton Postle, photo: Vauxhall Fashion Scout
59–65 Courtesy Markus Lupfer
67–73 Courtesy Irina Shaposhnikova, photographer: Boy Kortekaas, model: Seija Mistiaen
75–78 Victor Fraile/Getty Images
79–81 Shima Seiki MFG., Ltd.
83–87 CHRISTOPHER DADEY for SIBLING
88 THOMAS GIDDINGS for SIBLING
89 COZETTE MCCREERY for SIBLING
91–96 Courtesy Carlo Volpi; photography: Tracer Ital; hair stylist and makeup: Davide Barbieri; styling: Jenna Young; models: Blake and Marcel @ Oxygen
97 Courtesy Carlo Volpi
99 Courtesy Christian Wijnants, photo: Shoji Fuji
100–104 Courtesy Christian Wijnants, photo: Viviane Sassen
105 Courtesy Christian Wijnants
107–13 Image Courtesy of The Woolmark Company
117–23 © Ute Lennartz-Lembeck www.ute-lennartz-lembeck.de
125–26, 128–31 Courtesy Isabel Berglund, photo: Christoffer Askman
127 (top) Courtesy Isabel Berglund, photo: Erling Lykke Jeppesen
127 (bottom) Photo: Isabel Berglund
133 Courtesy Liz Collins, photo: Delia Kovac
134 Courtesy Liz Collins, photo: Arthi Sundaresh
135 Courtesy Liz Collins, photo: Cesar Lechowick
136 Courtesy Liz Collins, photo: Marc Lester
137 Courtesy Liz Collins, photo: Daphne Fitzpatrick
138 Courtesy Liz Collins, photo: Amy Fries
139 Courtesy Liz Collins, photo: Corey Greyhorse
141–42, 144, 146–47 Photo: Chia-Shan Lee
143, 145 Courtesy Chia-Shan Lee; photo: Takahito Sasaki; model: Gintare
149 Courtesy Ruth Marshall, photo: Robert Lowell
150 Courtesy Ruth Marshall, photo: James Daigle
151 Photo: Ruth Marshall
152–55 Courtesy Ruth Marshall, photo: Robert Lowell
157–63 © Lauren O'Farrell 2013
165–71 Namarietti by Na'ama Rietti
173, 175 Courtesy Magda Sayeg, photo: Mike Piscitelli
174, 178 Courtesy Magda Sayeg, photo: Magda Sayeg
176 Courtesy Magda Sayeg, photo: Shawn Thomas
177 Courtesy Magda Sayeg
179 (top) Courtesy Magda Sayeg, photo: Cesar Ortega
179 (bottom) Courtesy Magda Sayeg, photo: Ben Sayeg
181, 184–87 Courtesy Annette Streyl, photo: Ulrich Gehner
182 Courtesy Annette Streyl, photo: Helmut Kunde
183 Courtesy Annette Streyl, photo: Michael Plisterer
191, 192 (right), 193, 195 © Annette Bugansky, photo: Sussie Ahlburg
192 (left), 194, 196–97 © Annette Bugansky, photo: Annette Bugansky
199 Courtesy of Enel Contemporanea, photo: Eliot Wright
200–201 Courtesy of Enel Contemporanea, photo: Roberto Boccaccino
202–3, 205 Courtesy Charles MacAdam, photo: Masaki Koizumi
204 Courtesy Charles MacAdam, photo: Charles MacAdam
207 Bainain by Claire Anne O'Brien, courtesy Claire Anne O'Brien
208–9 Casta by Claire Anne O'Brien 2013 for Happen Projects, photo: Daniel Martinek
210–11 Fite by Claire Anne O'Brien, photo: Matt Robinson
212 (top) Sample Piece by Claire Anne O'Brien, photo: Claire Anne O'Brien
212 (bottom) Studio by Claire Anne O'Brien, photo: Claire Anne O'Brien
213 (top) Cruinn by Claire Anne O'Brien, photo: Matt Robinson
213 (bottom) Cisean Beag by Claire Anne O'Brien, photo: Matt Robinson
215–21 Courtesy Catherine Tough, photo: Milton Ogakgole
223–26 Science Museum/Science & Society Picture Library
227–29 © Pat Ashforth & Steve Plummer
231, 232 (top) The Yarn Company
232 (bottom) The Yarn Company, Midnight in Manhattan, our exclusive Colorway from Madelinetosh. Photo: Madelinetosh
233 Rubik's Blanket, The Yarn Company Exclusive, Designer: Irina Poludnenko
234 Courtesy Laura Zukaite and The Yarn Company, photo: Marc Hall, model: Ashly Priest
235 The Yarn Company Exclusive, Designer: Irina Poludnenko
236–37 The Yarn Company